ILLUSTRATED LIBRARY OF COOKING

VOLUME 14 San-Sea

*Everything you need to know
about sandwiches—the hot
and the cold, the plain and the
party . . . The fundamentals
of making sauces and gravies
for meats and vegetables . . .
AND an entire cookbook
devoted to seafood. That's
what Volume 14 has in store.
There's something for every
cook no matter how inex-
perienced or accomplished.*

ROCKVILLE HOUSE PUBLISHERS, INC.
ROCKVILLE CENTRE, NEW YORK 11570

VOLUME 14

Family Circle®

Illustrated Library of

COOKING

YOUR READY REFERENCE FOR A LIFETIME OF GOOD EATING

Picture Credits:

Foods from France • The International Shrimp Council • George Nordhausen • Peanut Growers of Georgia and Alabama • Pepperidge Farm • Planters Peanut Oil

Table of Contents

A peanut butter and lettuce sandwich made with whole wheat bread, soup, a fruit and milk are both a hearty and wholesome lunch.

1670

A triple-decker hero—sliced tomatoes on lettuce on sliced Swiss cheese on ham on sesame rolls, then *pickles, cheese, salami.*

SANDWICHES—OPEN AND SHUT

SANDWICHES—OPEN AND SHUT: OLD FAVORITES AND NEW TWISTS, CLUBS AND DAGWOODS, DANISH AND OTHER OPEN-FACE SANDWICHES, HEROES AND HOBOES, DAINTY PARTY SANDWICHES

Some like them hot, some like them cold. Some like them open, some like them shut. Some like them plain, some like them fancy—piled high, in fact, with wild conglomerations of fillings. "Them," as you have no doubt guessed, are sandwiches.

They owe their name to England's Fourth Earl of Sandwich (John Montagu, 1718-1792) who was so devoted to gambling he refused to leave the gaming tables even to eat. So a clever chef devised a way of serving him "at table," using slices of bread as plates because they, like the cold slices of roast resting between them, were edible.

Still earlier versions of sandwiches—open-face—can be traced to medieval Scandinavia when meals were spooned upon sturdy slices of bread. The open-face idea persists and, indeed, "Danish" sandwiches have become popular throughout America.

In the pages that follow, you'll discover dozens of recipes for all manner of sandwiches, both domestic and foreign. There are the many-decker Dagwoods and clubs, the hot and savory heroes, the artistic Danish. There's also a special section on making and decorating dainty party sandwiches, many of them looking for all the world like pastel *petits fours*.

SOME SANDWICH-MAKING TIPS

• For variety, take advantage of all the inviting flavors and shapes of breads, rolls and buns that are available today. And once in a while put some fun in your job and the lunch box, too, by using two kinds of bread for a sandwich—whole wheat and white, or white and rye, for example. Just be sure to choose slices of the same size and shape so the edges will fit together neatly.

• To keep fillings from soaking into the bread, spread the butter or margarine all the way to the crusts.

• For easy spreading without tearing bread, always soften regular or whipped butter or margarine first, or depend on soft margarine. Another trick is to freeze the bread first; then the butter spreads like a dream.

• No need to trim the crusts from bread except on the daintiest sandwiches. Crusts will help keep the edges of the bread from drying out and curling.

• For speed when you're making a big batch of sandwiches, use the assembly-line technique;

1671

that is, line up the bread slices, two by two, in rows on your counter top, keeping them in order as they come from the loaf.

• When making sandwiches "to go," pack lettuce and cucumber slices so they'll stay crisp and fresh this way: Wrap them loosely in wet paper toweling, then bundle into a transparent sandwich bag. Come lunchtime, they can be added to the sandwich. Raw relishes also travel neatly in a transparent bag.

• For easy eating, cut sandwiches for youngsters into 4 small wedges, squares or strips.

• Set aside a shelf in your cupboard to hold lunch-packing materials—wax paper, foil, transparent wrap and bags and paper napkins; a variety of containers and cups in various sizes and shapes; and plastic knives, forks and spoons. They'll all save you steps and time when you're rushed; some are a help in keeping foods neat and making toting easy.

TIPS ON FREEZING SANDWICHES

• Choose a time when your kitchen is not busy and make and wrap enough sandwiches for a week or two at the most. Sandwiches start to lose their fresh flavor if frozen longer.

• All breads and rolls freeze well, so look for variety. As a rule of thumb, figure about 18 slices of bread in a 1-pound loaf. Again, be sure to butter bread right to the edges to prevent the filling from soaking in.

• Avoid fillings with watery raw vegetables—lettuce, tomato, celery, cucumber; spreads such as jelly or jam; mayonnaise or salad dressing; and hard-cooked egg whites.

• Dairy sour cream, milk, pineapple or orange juice, applesauce and cream cheese are all good binders for sandwich fillings to be frozen.

• Cut each sandwich into convenient pieces and package tightly in moisture- and vaporproof paper; label, date and freeze.

1672

• Pack sandwiches into the lunch box directly from the freezer. They will be thawed and fresh-tasting by lunchtime.

SOME FAVORITE SANDWICH FILLINGS

Note: These all freeze well.

• Ground Roast beef, lamb, pork, ham, veal or chicken moistened with gravy and seasoned with grated onion, prepared horseradish or Worcestershire sauce.

• Chopped cooked chicken livers or calf's or lamb liver mixed with mashed hard-cooked egg yolk, minced onion and catsup.

• Cream cheese, chopped stuffed olives and salted peanuts moistened with undiluted evaporated milk.

• Mashed sardines, lemon juice and grated cheese.

• Sliced tongue and American cheese with mustard pickle.

• Sliced roast lamb on bread spread with mint-seasoned butter. (Cream 1 stick butter or margarine with 1 tablespoon chopped fresh mint.)

• Peanut butter and honey; peanut butter and crisp bacon bits; peanut butter and applesauce; peanut butter and sliced sweet pickle.

• Canned corned beef or liver spread seasoned with grated onion, chopped pickle or chili sauce.

• Sliced meat loaf, sliced Swiss cheese and mustard.

• Chopped hard-cooked egg yolks, crisp bacon bits, grated onion and catsup.

• Deviled ham, chopped mustard pickle, and mashed hard-cooked egg yolks.

• Ground cooked ham, ground Cheddar cheese, minced onion and chili sauce.

• Canned tuna on bread spread with savory butter. (Cream 1 stick butter or margarine with 2 tablespoons catsup, mustard-pickle relish or tomato-pickle relish.)

• Chopped cooked chicken, chopped salted almonds and cream cheese softened with milk.

• Thinly sliced frankfurters with baked beans and mustard-pickle relish.

• Chili con carne and chopped onion.

• Cream cheese and blue cheese (equal parts) moistened with milk.

OLD FAVORITES, NEW TWISTS

Peanut-Butter Towers
Team peanut butter—crunchy or cream style—with ripe tomatoes and old-fashioned pickles.
Makes 6 servings

Spread 6 slices white or whole-wheat bread generously with peanut butter; top with a layer of drained bread-and-butter pickles, pressing them slightly into peanut butter. Spread another 6 slices bread with mayonnaise; cover with salt and pepper. Put peanut-butter-spread slices on top, sandwich style; cut each sandwich into quarters.

Cheese Dreams

Easiest way we know to make a lot of sandwiches in a hurry.
Bake at 500° about 5 minutes. Makes 6 servings

½ cup (1 stick) butter or margarine, melted
12 slices white bread
12 slices process American cheese

1 Cut clean brown paper to fit a large cookie sheet; brush generously with melted butter or margarine.
2 Lay 6 slices bread in single layer on buttered paper; top each with 2 slices cheese and another slice bread; cut in half; brush tops with remaining melted butter or margarine.
3 Bake in very hot oven (500°) about 5 minutes, or until tops are golden-brown and cheese is melted.
4 Lift from paper with pancake turner; serve piping hot.

If you quarter a ''Dagwood,'' the eating is much easier.

Grilled Cheese for a Crowd

Bake at 500° for 5 minutes. Makes 12 servings

½ cup mayonnaise or salad dressing
¼ cup finely chopped dill pickle
24 slices white bread
3 packages (8 ounces each) sliced provolone cheese
½ cup (1 stick) butter or margarine melted

1 Mix mayonnaise or salad dressing and pickle in a small bowl; spread 1 rounded teaspoonful on each slice of bread.
2 Place cheese on half the bread slices, cutting cheese to fit; top with remaining bread, spread side down. Brush sandwiches lightly on both sides with melted butter or margarine; place on cookie sheets.
3 Bake in extremely hot oven (500°) 5 minutes, or until golden and cheese is melted. (No need to turn.) Cut in half diagonally; serve hot.

Melty Mix-Ups

Eat 'em hot right from their foil jackets.
Bake at 400° for 15 minutes. Makes 6 servings

1 can (12 ounces) pork luncheon meat
1 cup grated process Swiss cheese (half an 8-ounce package)
2 hard-cooked eggs, diced
¼ cup mayonnaise
1 tablespoon grated onion
½ teaspoon dry mustard
6 hamburger buns, split

1 Mash pork luncheon meat with a fork in medium-size bowl; stir in cheese, eggs, mayonnaise, onion and mustard.
2 Spoon into prepared rolls; wrap each in aluminum foil, sealing tightly; place on cookie sheet.
3 Bake in hot oven (400°) about 15 minutes, or until heated through.

Baked Puff Sandwiches

Bake at 350° for 45 minutes. Makes 4 servings

1 can (12 ounces) pork luncheon meat
2 tablespoons bottled sandwich spread
8 slices slightly dry bread, buttered and crusts removed
3 eggs
2 cups milk
1 small onion, grated
1 tablespoon prepared mustard

1 Break up meat with fork; mix with sandwich spread; spread between bread slices to make four sandwiches; halve diagonally; arrange in single layer in shallow baking dish, 11x7x2.
2 Beat eggs slightly in small bowl; blend in milk, onion and mustard; spoon over sandwiches; chill for at least 1 hour.
3 Bake in moderate oven (350°) about 45 minutes, or until top is puffed and golden; serve at once.

1673

Triangle Crisps

Makes 4 sandwiches

8 slices thin-sliced white bread
1 carton (4 ounces) whipped cream cheese

½ cup chopped raw spinach
4 radishes, thinly sliced
1 small carrot, scraped and cut into thin sticks

1 Spread bread with whipped cream cheese; sprinkle chopped spinach over 4 slices; top each with a layer of radishes and carrot sticks.
2 Put bread together to make 4 sandwiches; slice each into 2 triangles.

Ham-Salad Triangles
Fix these sandwiches ahead, if you like, cover, and chill.
Makes 6 servings

2 cups finely diced cooked ham
½ cup finely diced celery
1 teaspoon grated onion
⅓ cup mayonnaise or salad dressing
1 teaspoon prepared mustard
12 thin slices white bread, buttered

1 Mix ham, celery, onion, mayonnaise or salad dressing and mustard in a medium-size bowl.
2 Spread bread with ham-salad mixture to make 6 sandwiches; trim crusts, if you wish.
3 Cut each sandwich diagonally into quarters; arrange on bread-and-butter plates on trays.

Grilled Tuna Sandwiches
Just watch everyone go for this French toast variation of the tuna-salad favorite.
Makes 6 sandwiches

2 cans (about 7 ounces each) tuna, drained and flaked
½ cup diced Swiss cheese
¼ cup finely chopped celery
¼ cup toasted slivered almonds (from a 5-ounce can)
½ cup mayonnaise or salad dressing
1 tablespoon lemon juice
1 teaspoon Worcestershire sauce
1 teaspoon prepared mustard
12 slices white bread
3 eggs
½ cup milk
½ teaspoon salt
Butter or margarine

1 Mix tuna, diced cheese, celery, almonds, mayonnaise or salad dressing, lemon juice, Worcestershire sauce and mustard in a medium-size bowl.
2 Spread about ½ cup on each of 6 of the bread slices; put together with remaining bread to make 6 sandwiches. (Sandwiches may be made ahead and chilled, if you wish.)

3 Beat eggs slightly with milk and salt in a pie plate. Dip sandwiches, one at a time, into mixture, turning to soak both sides well.
4 Sauté slowly, turning once, in butter or margarine until golden in a large frying pan or on an electric grill or griddle. Serve piping-hot.

Deep-Sea Stacks
As simple as layering tuna salad between crisp cucumbers on bread spread with curry butter.
Makes 4 servings

6 tablespoons (¾ stick) butter or margarine
½ teaspoon curry powder
8 slices bread
1 can (about 7 ounces) tuna, drained and flaked
¼ cup mayonnaise or salad dressing
Salt and pepper
1 medium-size cucumber, pared and sliced thin

1 Blend butter and curry powder in small bowl; spread on bread slices.
2 Combine tuna and mayonnaise or salad dressing in small bowl; season with salt and pepper.
3 Layer each of 4 slices of bread this way: Cucumber slices, tuna mixture and cucumber slices, dividing evenly. Top with remaining bread slices, butter side down.
4 Slice each in half crosswise; garnish with carrot curls, if you wish.

Pâté Supper Sandwiches
Makes 6 servings

½ pound sliced bacon
1 pound chicken livers
2 tablespoons chopped onion
1 can (3 or 4 ounces) sliced mushrooms
1¼ teaspoons salt
2 teaspoons Worcestershire sauce
4 tablespoons (½ stick) butter or margarine
3 medium-size tomatoes, sliced thin
2 teaspoons sugar
¼ teaspoon pepper
¼ cup chopped parsley
12 large slices rye bread

1 Sauté bacon until crisp in a medium-size frying pan; remove and drain on paper toweling; keep warm. Pour all drippings from pan, then measure 2 tablespoonfuls and return to pan.
2 Stir chicken livers and onion into pan. Cook slowly, stirring constantly, 5 minutes, or until browned; stir in mushrooms and liquid, ¼ teaspoon of the salt and Worcestershire sauce.

Teenagers and tweenagers (between grammar school and high school) go for Barbecue Bunburgers and Rivieras.

Cook, stirring several times, 5 minutes, or until liquid evaporates. Mash mixture well with a fork.
3 While livers cook, melt butter or margarine in a shallow baking pan; place tomatoes in a single layer in pan; sprinkle with sugar, remaining 1 teaspoon salt and pepper.
4 Heat in moderate oven (350°) 5 minutes, or just until hot; sprinkle with parsley.
5 Place each of 6 slices of bread on a serving plate; top with tomatoes, then drizzle buttery drippings from pan over tomatoes. Spread liver mixture over tomatoes, dividing evenly. Top with bacon and remaining bread slices. Cut each

sandwich in half; serve hot with potato chips and dill pickles, if you wish.

Barbecue Bunburgers
Quick contents: Barbecue filling from a can, cheese from a package.
Heat rolls at 400° for 10 minutes, bake sandwiches at 400° for 5 minutes. Makes 6 sandwiches

6 oblong hard rolls
1 large onion, peeled and sliced

1 large green pepper, seeded and diced
4 tablespoons (½ stick) butter or margarine
1 can (about 1 pound) barbecue sauce with beef
1 package (8 ounces) sliced process American cheese, cut in strips
2 cups shredded iceberg lettuce

1 Cut a thin slice from tops, then hollow out rolls. Place rolls and tops on a cookie sheet. Heat in hot oven (400°) 10 minutes, or until toasted.
2 Sauté onion and green pepper in butter or margarine until soft in a medium-size frying pan; stir in beef mixture; heat until bubbly. Spoon into hollows in rolls; top with cheese strips.
3 Bake in hot oven (400°) 5 minutes, or until cheese melts. Cover each with shredded lettuce and top of roll. Serve hot.

Super Burgers
One's a generous serving—each patty is made with 6 ounces of meat.
Makes 4 servings

1½ pounds ground beef
1 small onion, grated
1 tablespoon bottled steak sauce
1 teaspoon salt
¼ teaspoon pepper
3 slices process Swiss cheese, cut into thin strips
4 hamburger buns, split, toasted and buttered
Lettuce
4 thick slices tomato
Mayonnaise
Onion rings
Red-pepper relish

1 Combine beef, onion, steak sauce, salt and pepper in medium-size bowl; mix lightly with a fork; shape into 4 thick patties.
2 Broil, following range manufacturer's directions, about 8 minutes on one side; turn; crisscross cheese strips on top, dividing evenly; broil about 5 minutes longer, or until cheese is melted and meat is done as you like it.
3 Place a halved bun on each serving plate; top one half with lettuce, then tomato slice; spread with mayonnaise; add broiled meat patty; garnish with a few onion rings and a generous spoonful of red-pepper relish.

Rivieras
Ham and chicken, French-toasted, with mayonnaise-cranberry sauce to top it off.
Makes 6 sandwiches

½ cup (1 stick) butter or margarine
12 half-inch-thick slices French bread
12 slices cooked chicken
1 package (6 ounces) sliced boiled ham
3 eggs
¾ cup milk
1 cup mayonnaise or salad dressing
1 can (8 ounces) whole-fruit cranberry sauce

1 Spread half of the butter or margarine on bread; make into 6 sandwiches with chicken and ham, dividing evenly.
2 Beat eggs slightly with milk in a pie plate; dip sandwiches into mixture, turning to coat both sides well. Brown slowly in remaining butter or margarine, turning once, in a large frying pan.
3 Blend mayonnaise or salad dressing with cranberry sauce in a small bowl. Serve sandwiches hot with dressing.

Juarez Turkey Buns
Makes 4 sandwiches

3 tablespoons butter or margarine
1 teaspoon chili powder
1 can (about 1 pound) red kidney beans, drained
1 tablespoon mayonnaise or salad dressing
¾ teaspoon salt
4 hamburger buns, split
2 packages (3 ounces each) sliced turkey
1⅓ cups finely shredded iceberg lettuce
¼ cup finely chopped sweet red pepper

1 Melt 1 tablespoon of the butter or margarine in a small frying pan; stir in chili powder; cook 1 minute.
2 Mash kidney beans in a medium-size bowl; stir in chili mixture, mayonnaise or salad dressing and salt.
3 Toast hamburger buns lightly; spread with remaining 2 tablespoons butter or margarine. Spread bean mixture on each of 4 halves; top with turkey slices, then with lettuce, red pepper and remaining bun halves, buttered side down. Serve with green-onion-flavor corn chips, if you wish.

Meat Loaf Lineup
Bake meat loaf at 375° for 55 minutes. Makes 6 servings

1 pound ground beef
1 egg
1 can (8 ounces) tomato sauce
½ cup fine dry bread crumbs
1 envelope (about 1½ ounces) spaghetti sauce mix
1 loaf Italian bread
1 teaspoon leaf oregano, crumbled
6 tablespoons (¾ stick) butter or margarine, melted
1 tablespoon grated Parmesan cheese
1 can or jar (4 ounces) whole pimientos, drained

1 Combine ground beef, egg, tomato sauce, bread crumbs and spaghetti sauce mix in a medium-size bowl; mix lightly until well blended. Press into a loaf pan, 8x4x2.
2 Bake in moderate oven (375°) 55 minutes, or until crusty-brown.
3 Cut bread into 24 slices, keeping slices in order. Stir oregano into melted butter or margarine; brush over slices; put back in loaf shape. Brush outside of loaf with remaining butter mixture; sprinkle with cheese. Wrap loaf in foil. Heat in oven with meat loaf 10 minutes, or until hot.
4 Remove meat loaf from pan; cut into 12 slices; place 1 slice between each two slices of bread. Slit each pimiento down side to make two pieces; tuck alongside alternate slices of meat; tuck green-onion ruffles beside remaining slices, if you wish.

Bavarian Beef Plate
Relishlike sauerkraut tops corned beef and cheese on zesty pumpernickel.
Makes 4 servings

1 can (1 pound) sauerkraut, well drained and chopped
½ cup bottled Thousand Island dressing
8 large slices pumpernickel, buttered
1 package (8 ounces) sliced Muenster cheese
1 can (12 ounces) corned beef, cut into 8 slices
Dill pickles, sliced
Spiced crab apples

1 Mix sauerkraut and Thousand Island dressing in a small bowl.
2 Place 1 slice of bread on each of 4 serving plates; top each with cheese, then corned beef.
3 Spoon sauerkraut mixture over corned beef; cover with remaining slices of bread. Hold in place with wooden picks topped with pickle slices. Cut each sandwich in half. Garnish plates with spiced crab apples.

Meat Loaf Lineups and coffee: perfect TV accompaniment.

Milwaukee Jumbos
On rye bread, a bonus: Spread of sour cream and onion dip mix.
Makes 6 sandwiches

3 packages (4 ounces each) sliced corned beef
1 can (1 pound) sauerkraut
¾ cup dairy sour cream
1 packet (2 to an envelope) onion dip mix
12 large slices rye bread

1 Unwrap corned beef, then rewrap lightly in foil. Place packet on top of sauerkraut in a medium-size saucepan; cover. Simmer 10 minutes.
2 Blend sour cream and dip mix in a cup; spread on bread.
3 Place corned beef, dividing evenly, on half the bread slices. Drain sauerkraut and spoon over corned beef; cover with remaining bread, spread side down. Serve warm.

Pocketbook Hotdogs
Bake biscuits at 450° for 12 minutes. Makes 4 servings

2 cups biscuit mix
Milk
1 cup shredded process American cheese
4 frankfurters
4 slices bacon, cooked and crumbled

1677

2 tablespoons butter or margarine
2 tablespoons prepared mustard

1 Prepare biscuit mix with milk, following label directions for rolled biscuits; stir in ⅓ cup of the cheese.
2 Turn dough out onto a lightly floured pastry cloth or board; knead several times, or until smooth. Pat out to a rectangle, 6x5; cut cross-wise into 4 pieces. Place on a cookie sheet.
3 Bake in very hot oven (450°) 12 minutes, or until golden. Remove from oven; raise temperature to BROIL.
4 While biscuits bake, heat frankfurters in water, following label directions; drain. Mix remaining cheese and bacon in a small bowl.
5 Split biscuits lengthwise almost through; spread with butter or margarine, then mustard. Place a frankfurter in each biscuit; sprinkle with bacon mixture. Return to cookie sheet.
6 Broil, 4 to 5 inches from heat, 1 minute, or until cheese melts. Serve hot.

Frankfurter Bunwiches

Plump hotdogs, creamy coleslaw and rolls come ready-fixed—just put together and heat.
Bake at 450° for 15 minutes. Makes 8 servings

8 split frankfurter rolls
½ cup prepared sandwich spread
8 frankfurters (about 1 pound)
1 jar (1 pound) coleslaw

1 Spread rolls with sandwich spread; place a frankfurter in each, then spoon coleslaw on top, dividing evenly.
2 Wrap each sandwich in a square of foil; seal tightly. Place on cookie sheet.
3 Bake in very hot oven (450°) 15 minutes, or until hot. Fold foil back; serve sandwiches in wrappers.

Hot Steak Bunwiches

Flank steak is an easy cut to carve for sandwiches as it's all meat. Broil it fast for tender juicy perfection.
Makes 6 to 8 servings, 2 buns each

1 flank steak (about 2 pounds)
Salt and pepper
12 to 16 split BUTTER-CRISP HERB BUNS (recipe follows)

1 Make shallow diagonal cuts 1 inch apart on one side of steak (to keep meat from curling); place, scored side down, on broiler rack.
2 Broil, following range-manufacturer's directions, 3 minutes; turn; broil 3 to 4 minutes longer

1678

for rare meat; season with salt and pepper; cut at once on the diagonal into thin slices. (If meat has to stand, keep slices close together, like uncut steak, to hold in juices.)
3 To serve, fold each slice in half, pop into a split hot bun.

Butter-Crisp Herb Buns

A surprise ingredient—instant powdered cream—gives rolls a thin shattery crust.
Bake at 350° for 20 minutes. Makes 18 rolls

¼ cup vegetable shortening
½ teaspoon ground nutmeg
½ teaspoon leaf oregano, crumbled
¼ teaspoon leaf basil, crumbled
2 packages active dry yeast
¼ cup warm water
4¼ cups sifted all-purpose flour
¼ cup instant powdered cream
¼ cup sugar
2 teaspoons salt
2 eggs, beaten
1 cup water
3 tablespoons butter or margarine, melted

1 Melt vegetable shortening with nutmeg, oregano and basil in small saucepan; cool.
2 Dissolve yeast in warm water in large bowl; stir in cooled shortening mixture, 2 cups flour, instant powdered cream, sugar, salt, eggs and water; beat with wooden spoon; gradually beat in remaining flour to form a stiff dough.
3 Knead on lightly floured pastry cloth or board about 5 minutes, or until smooth and satiny; shape into a ball.
4 Place dough in greased large bowl; brush top with butter or margarine; cover with clean towel; let rise in warm place, away from draft, 1½ hours, or until double in bulk.
5 Punch down dough; turn out onto lightly floured pastry cloth or board; roll out to ½-inch thickness; cut out rounds with a 2½-inch cookie cutter; knead trimmings, roll and cut out to make a total of 18 rounds; arrange in greased jelly-roll pan, 15x10x1;* brush with melted butter or margarine; cover with clean towel; let rise in warm place, away from draft, about 30 minutes, or until double in bulk.
6 Bake in moderate oven (350°) 20 minutes, or until golden-brown; turn out onto wire racks; serve hot.

* Or make only 9 buns with half the dough; bake in a greased square pan, 9x9x2. Shape remaining dough into a loaf; place in buttered loaf pan, 9x5x3; let rise 1 hour; bake 45 minutes, or until bread pulls away from sides of pan.

Steak Rolls
Flavored tenderizer, easy hollandaise make beef chuck steak-house good.
Makes 6 sandwiches

1 chuck beefsteak, cut 1 inch thick (about 1½ pounds)
  Instant seasoned meat tenderizer
2 packages hollandaise sauce mix
  Milk or water
3 round hard rolls, split, toasted and buttered

1 Moisten steak and sprinkle with tenderizer, following label directions. Place on rack in broiler pan.
2 Prepare hollandaise sauce mix with milk or water, following label directions; keep warm.
3 Broil steak, following range manufacturer's directions, 8 minutes on each side for medium-rare, or until as done as you like it. Remove to a cutting board; carve diagonally in ½-inch-thick slices.
4 Place each half roll on a serving plate; top with several slices of steak; spoon hollandaise sauce over all. Serve hot.

CLUBS AND DAGWOODS

Simple Salmon Jumbos
Layers of salmon salad, crisp cucumber, hard-cooked egg, tomatoes and toast stack up to this meatless hearty.
Makes 4 sandwiches

 1 can (about 8 ounces) salmon, drained, boned and flaked
¼ cup mayonnaise or salad dressing
 1 teaspoon lemon juice
¼ teaspoon salt
 1 large cucumber, pared
12 slices white bread, toasted and buttered
 2 medium-size tomatoes, sliced
 4 hard-cooked eggs, shelled and sliced
 4 large pitted ripe olives, each cut in 4 slices

1 Combine salmon, mayonnaise or salad dressing, lemon juice and salt in a small bowl.
2 Cut a 2-inch-long piece from cucumber; set aside for garnish in Step 4; slice remaining.
3 Layer each of 4 buttered toast slices this way:

Simple Salmon Jumbos are super sandwich sky-scrapers.

Salmon mixture, cucumber slices, toast, tomato and egg slices; top with remaining toast, buttered side down. Press wooden picks into sandwiches to hold in place; cut each sandwich diagonally into quarters.

4 Cut saved cucumber into matchlike strips; thread several through each olive slice; place on picks.

●

Grilled Tuna-Cheese Stacks

Bake at 400° for 10 to 12 minutes. Makes 6 servings

  1 can (about 7 ounces) tuna, drained and flaked
  1 package (5 ounces) frozen deveined cooked shrimps, thawed
  ½ cup diced celery
  1 pimiento, cut in thin strips
  ¼ teaspoon salt
  ⅛ teaspoon pepper
  ½ cup dairy sour cream
  ¼ cup mayonnaise or salad dressing
18 slices bread
  ¼ cup (½ stick) melted butter or margarine
  3 tomatoes, sliced
  2 tablespoons grated onion
  ¼ pound (1 cup) grated sharp Cheddar cheese

1 Combine tuna, shrimps, celery, pimiento, salt, pepper, sour cream and mayonnaise or salad dressing in medium-size bowl; mix lightly.
2 Trim crusts from sliced bread; brush with melted butter or margarine; put together to make 6 three-decker sandwiches with tuna-shrimp mixture for one filling, tomato slices and grated onion for the second; sprinkle tops with grated cheese; place on cookie sheet.
3 Bake in hot oven (400°) 10 to 12 minutes, or until cheese melts.

●

All-American Club

The aristocrat of sandwiches—a three-decker of buttery toast with meat, cheese and tomato. Makes 4 servings

12 slices white or whole-wheat bread, toasted and buttered
   Lettuce
  8 slices ripe tomatoes
12 slices (about ½ pound) bacon, crisply cooked
  4 slices cooked ham

This is a sandwich? Twin Dagwoods on a Skewer!

4 slices process Swiss cheese
Prepared mustard or mayonnaise
Stuffed olives
Sweet gherkins

1 Arrange 4 slices buttered toast in a row; top each with lettuce, 2 slices tomato and 3 strips bacon; add a second slice of toast, then lettuce and a slice each of ham and cheese.
2 Spread remaining toast with mustard or mayonnaise; lay, spread side down, on top of cheese; insert 4 wooden picks into each sandwich to hold it together; cut each diagonally into 4 triangles; stick olives and gherkins onto ends of wooden picks.

Champ
Makes 2 or 3 servings

1 long loaf (about 16 inches)
    Italian bread
    Softened butter or margarine
6 slices (from 8-ounce package) process
    American cheese
6 slices liverwurst
1 dill pickle, cut into 8 thin slices
2 bottled hot red peppers, sliced
    Lettuce, olive oil, vinegar, salt
6 slices bologna
6 slices salami
1 tomato, cut into 6 slices
    Sweet onion rings

1 Cut bread into three lengthwise slices; spread cut surfaces with softened butter or margarine.
2 Cover bottom slice with cheese, liverwurst, pickle and hot red peppers; top with middle slice of bread.
3 Begin second filling with lettuce; drizzle with olive oil and vinegar and sprinkle with salt; top with bologna, salami, tomato and onion rings; replace crust.
4 Cut loaf crosswise into halves or thirds; wrap each in a paper napkin to eat out of hand.

Bologna-Cheese Kebab Sandwich
Bake at 350° for 20 minutes. Makes 9 to 12 sandwiches

1 loaf Italian bread (14 to 16 inches lon)
½ cup (1 stick) butter or margarine
4 teaspoons horseradish mustard
2 to 3 packages (6 ounces each) thinly sliced
    bologna (16 to 24 slices)
12 stuffed olives, sliced
1 package (6 ounces) cubed Cheddar cheese

1 Cut pointed ends from bread, then cut into ½-inch slices this way: Make first cut almost through to bottom of loaf and second cut clear through; repeat (finished individual sandwiches will be separate this way).
2 Cream butter or margarine with horseradish mustard; spread generously between the hinged slices; place 2 folded slices of bologna in each "sandwich," half in and half poking out.
3 Run two skewers (1 from each end) through bread to hold it together; place on a large piece of aluminum foil on cookie sheet; arrange sliced olives, then cubed cheese down center; bring foil up and around loaf and seal tightly.
4 Bake in moderate oven (350°) 20 minutes, or until heated through and cheese is melted. Unwrap; remove skewers before serving. Each sandwich will pull apart easily; serve hot.

Twin Dagwoods on a Skewer
Each person gets two sandwiches—one with meats and the other with cheese.

Cut 1 long loaf of Italian or French bread in half, then cut each half into 8 slices, keeping them in order. Spread slices in pairs with softened butter or margarine. Fill first pair with sliced Muenster cheese folded around 1 or 2 thin tomato slices. Fill second pair with folded slices of bologna and salami tucked into romaine leaves. Repeat with remaining pairs, reforming loaf as each sandwich is made. Slip a thin slice of dill pickle between sandwiches; spear loaf with a long skewer to hold together. Makes 4 servings, 2 sandwiches each.

Milwaukee Stack-Ups
Men will love these huskies of meat, sauerkraut and cheese.
Makes 6 servings, 2 sandwiches each

½ cup mayonnaise
½ cup tomato-pickle relish
12 slices round pumpernickel bread
2 cans (12 ounces each) beef luncheon meat,
    cut into 24 thin slices
12 long slices process Swiss cheese (about ¾
    pound)
1 can (14 ounces) sauerkraut, well drained

1 Mix mayonnaise and tomato-pickle relish in 2-cup measure; spread generously over bread slices; halve each slice.
2 Place 2 slices of luncheon meat side by side on each slice of cheese; top with a spoonful of sauerkraut; fold meat and cheese over sauerkraut and pop between 2 half bread slices. Repeat to make 12 sandwiches.

1681

SANDWICHES—OPEN AND SHUT

Chicken-Cheese Clubs

Tomatoes and crisp cucumber make relishlike partners for bacon, chicken and Muenster.
Bake at 450° for 5 minutes. Makes 4 sandwiches

    12 slices bacon (½ pound)
     2 medium-size tomatoes, each cut in 4 slices
     ½ small cucumber, sliced
    12 slices whole-wheat bread, toasted and buttered
     ¼ cup prepared sandwich spread
     8 slices cooked chicken
     4 slices Muenster cheese (from an 8-ounce package)
     8 pitted ripe olives
     8 small sweet pickles

1 Sauté bacon until crisp in a large frying pan; drain on paper toweling.
2 Place tomato and cucumber slices and bacon, dividing evenly, on 4 pieces of the toast; add another slice of toast; spread with sandwich spread.
3 Top with chicken slices, then cheese and remaining toast, buttered side down. Place sandwiches on a cookie sheet.
4 Bake in very hot oven (450°) 5 minutes, or until cheese melts slightly.
5 Press wooden picks into sandwiches to hold in place; cut each sandwich diagonally into quarters. Top picks with olives and pickles.

Club Tower

Triple-deck sandwiches always make a hit. Filling calls for liverwurst, minced ham and chicken or turkey.
Makes 6 servings

    12 slices square white bread
     6 slices square whole-wheat bread
       Butter or margarine
     1 jar (5 ounces) smoky cheese spread
       Leaf lettuce
     1 package (6 ounces) sliced liverwurst
     1 package (6 ounces) sliced minced ham
     3 medium-size tomatoes, sliced thin
     1 package (5 ounces) sliced chicken or turkey
     1 bunch radishes, trimmed
     2 cans (about 2 ounces each) potato sticks

1 Toast bread. Spread white slices with butter or margarine and whole-wheat slices with cheese spread.
2 Layer each of 6 slices white toast this way: Lettuce; liverwurst; minced ham; whole-wheat toast, cheese side up; tomato slices; chicken

or turkey; white toast, buttered side down. Hold in place with wooden picks; place on serving plates. Garnish with radishes.
3 Cut each sandwich diagonally into 4 triangles. Serve with potato sticks.

Ham-and-Egg Towers

Six layers of bread are filled with ham and egg salad, then frosted with cream cheese.
Makes 8 sandwiches

     6 hard-cooked eggs, shelled and chopped
     ½ cup diced celery
     ½ cup mayonnaise or salad dressing
     ½ teaspoon prepared mustard
     ½ teaspoon salt
     1 cup ground cooked ham
     2 packages (8 ounces each) cream cheese, softened
     6 tablespoons light cream or table cream
    12 slices round white bread
     ½ cup chopped parsley

1 Mix chopped eggs, celery, mayonnaise or salad dressing, mustard and salt in a medium-size bowl.
2 Blend ground ham, half of one package of the cream cheese, and 1 tablespoon of the cream until smooth in a small bowl. Place remaining cream cheese and cream in a medium-size bowl; set aside for Step 4.
3 Spread egg-salad mixture on 6 slices of the bread and ham on 4 slices. Stack slices, alternating egg with ham, in 2 piles of 5 each; top with remaining bread slices.
4 Blend cream cheese and cream in bowl until smooth; spread over each sandwich stack to frost completely. Pat parsley on tops and sides to cover. Chill several hours.
5 When ready to serve, cut each stack into quarters with a very sharp knife. Garnish with dill-pickle wheels and serve with radish roses, if you wish. To make dill-pickle wheels, shave thin strips from medium-size dill pickles with a vegetable parer. Roll strips, then bunch 3 together; wrap another strip around all to hold them in place.

Chicken-Liver Bounties

Here's a sandwich to please gourmets. Cook livers ever so gently, then combine with broiled tomatoes and crisp bacon.
Makes 6 sandwiches

     6 slices bacon
     1 pound chicken livers
     2 tablespoons all-purpose flour
     ¼ teaspoons seasoned salt

5 Place 2 tomato slices on each bun half; spoon hot liver mixture over, dividing evenly. Top each with another tomato slice; sprinkle with crumbled bacon. Garnish with parsley, if you wish.

●

Zigzag Sandwich Loaf
Bake at 425° for 15 minutes. Makes 6 servings

  1 *loaf French bread*
  ¼ *cup melted butter or margarine*
  2 *tablespoons pickle relish*
  1 *tablespoon prepared mustard*
 12 *slices (about ½ pound) bologna*
  ¼ *pound process American cheese, cut in 1-inch strips*

1 Cut bread diagonally into 6 thick slices almost through to bottom crust; turn loaf end for end; slice same way again to make zigzag cuts completely across top.
2 Combine melted butter or margarine, pickle relish and mustard; brush between slices; fill cuts in bread with folded bologna slices and cheese strips (have cheese overlap crust so it will melt over top); wrap loaf loosely in aluminum foil; seal.
3 Bake in hot oven (425°) 10 minutes; open foil wrapper and fold back; bake 5 minutes longer, or until cheese is golden-brown and slightly melted. Serve hot.

DANISH AND OTHER OPEN-FACE SANDWICHES

Appian Sampler
Inspired by popular Italian antipasto, this sandwich combines a variety of food.
Makes 4 servings

  1 *small loaf Italian bread, cut into 16 slices*
  ⅓ *cup bottled Italian salad dressing*
    Romaine
  4 *medium-size tomatoes, each cut in 6 thin slices*
  2 *packages (6 ounces each) assorted sliced cold cuts*
  4 *slices provolone cheese, halved (from an 8-ounce package)*
  8 *large fresh mushrooms, washed, trimmed and sliced thin*
    OR: 1 can (3 or 4 ounces) sliced mushrooms, drained

This isn't angel food cake but Ham-and-Egg Towers.

  1 *can (3 or 4 ounces) chopped mushrooms*
  3 *large tomatoes, each cut in 6 slices*
  3 *split large hamburger buns*

1 Sauté bacon just until crisp in a large frying pan; drain on paper toweling, then crumble. Drain off all drippings, then measure 2 tablespoons and return to pan. (Set bacon aside for Step 5.)
2 Halve chicken livers; snip out any veiny parts or skin with scissors. Shake livers with flour and seasoned salt in a paper bag to coat.
3 Brown slowly in drippings in frying pan; stir in mushrooms and liquid. Heat, stirring constantly, to boiling; cover. Simmer 3 minutes, or just until livers lose their pink color.
4 While livers cook, place tomato slices and bun halves in a single layer on rack in broiler pan. Broil 3 to 4 minutes, or until tomatoes are heated through and buns are toasted.

Appian Sampler, Italian favorite served Danish-style.

12 small green onions, washed and trimmed
   Watercress
   Corn chips
   Red and green pepper strips

1 Place 4 slices bread on each of 4 serving plates; drizzle with salad dressing; top with romaine.
2 Layer bread this way: Tomatoes, meat, tomatoes, cheese, meat and mushrooms; lay 3 green onions across top of each sandwich. Tuck sprigs of watercress between layers or around edge of plates. Garnish plates with corn chips and pepper strips. Serve with ripe and stuffed green olives, and additional salad dressing, if you wish.

Danish Beef Sandwiches

Cook a big roast so you'll have enough left to turn into these open-face huskies.
Makes 4 sandwiches

  4 tablespoons (½ stick) butter or margarine
  2 tablespoons prepared horseradish
  4 slices pumpernickel bread
12 thin slices roast beef
  1 jar (1 pound) sliced pickled beets, drained

1 Blend butter or margarine with horseradish in a small bowl; spread on bread slices.
2 Top each with a slice of beef, then a layer of beets; repeat to make 2 more layers of each. Garnish with parsley and serve with freshly ground pepper, if you wish.

Smorgasbord Sandwiches

This sandwich has everything: rye bread, tongue, caraway and blue cheeses, sardines, hard-cooked eggs and beets.
Makes 4 servings

8 slices thin light rye bread, buttered
  Iceberg lettuce
1 package (6 ounces) sliced cooked tongue
4 long slices caraway cheese (from an 8-ounce package), folded
4 cherry tomatoes, halved
  Watercress
1 can (about 4 ounces) sardines, drained
2 hard-cooked eggs, shelled and sliced
2 wedges (about 1 ounce each) blue cheese, crumbled

SANDWICHES—OPEN AND SHUT

1 jar (about 1 pound) sliced pickled beets, drained
1 can (about 4 ounces) French fried onions

1 Place 1 slice rye bread on each of 4 serving plates. Halve remaining 4 slices diagonally; arrange each 2 triangles around whole slices on plates; top all with several leaves of lettuce.
2 Layer tongue and cheese slices, cherry tomatoes and watercress on top of whole slices of bread. Place sardines on one of the triangles on each plate, and hard-cooked egg slices on the other; sprinkle crumbled blue cheese over eggs.
3 Spoon beets into lettuce cups at one side of sandwiches; sprinkle lightly with dillweed, if you wish, and serve with French fried onions.

Steak Medallions
Makes 4 servings

3 medium-size onions, peeled and sliced thin
2 medium-size green peppers, seeded and sliced into thin rings
4 tablespoons (½ stick) butter or margarine
4 cube steaks or individual boneless steaks, cut about ¼ inch thick
4 hero rolls
2 medium-size tomatoes, each cut in 8 slices
½ teaspoon seasoned salt
½ teaspoon seasoned pepper

Sizzling-hot Steak Medallions with all the trimmings.

1 Sauté onions and green peppers in 2 tablespoons of the butter or margarine until soft in a large frying pan; remove with a slotted spoon and keep warm.
2 Sauté steaks in same frying pan 2 minutes on each side, or until done as you like beef.
3 Split rolls almost through; open out flat. Spread with remaining 2 tablespoons butter or margarine; place on serving plates.
4 Place tomato slices and steaks on rolls; sprinkle with salt and pepper. Spoon onion mixture over steaks. Serve hot with corn chips and a cola beverage, if you wish.

Heidelbergs
Makes 4 servings

1 can (1 pound, 11 ounces) sauerkraut
1 tart apple, halved, cored and diced
3 tablespoons sugar
1 package (¾ pound) smoked sausage links
1 tablespoon butter or margarine
½ cup mayonnaise or salad dressing
½ cup chili sauce
1 teaspoon instant minced onion
½ cup grated Cheddar cheese
8 large slices caraway rye bread

1 Drain liquid from sauerkraut. Combine sauerkraut with apple and sugar in a medium-size saucepan; heat to boiling; cover. Simmer 15 minutes to blend flavors; drain.
2 Split sausages lengthwise; sauté in butter or margarine until lightly browned in a medium-size frying pan.
3 Blend mayonnaise or salad dressing with chili sauce, onion and cheese in a small bowl.
4 Place 2 slices of bread on each of 4 serving plates; spread each with part of the mayonnaise mixture. Layer sauerkraut, remaining mayonnaise mixture and sausages on top. Garnish each with a sprig of parsley and serve with sour pickles, if you wish.

Mock Pizza Loaf
Bake at 375° for 30 minutes. Makes 6 servings

1 pound sweet Italian sausages, sliced
1 large onion, peeled and sliced
1 can (8 ounces) tomato sauce with cheese
2 packages refrigerated crescent rolls
½ cup grated Parmesan cheese
½ cup sliced pitted ripe olives

1 Sauté sausages in a medium-size frying pan 10 minutes, or until lightly browned; remove with a slotted spoon and set aside. Drain all drip-

Ham-and-Caraway Foldovers and Sun-Glow Salad make a sensational sandwich duo for an original luncheon.

pings from pan, then measure 2 tablespoonfuls and return to pan.

2 Stir in onion; sauté until soft. Stir in tomato sauce and sausage; heat slowly until bubbly.

3 Separate crescent rolls to make 4 rectangles; place, slightly overlapping, on a large cookie sheet. Roll out to a large rectangle, ¼ inch thick; sprinkle with grated cheese.

4 Spread sauce mixture over middle of dough, leaving a 3-inch border on each side; sprinkle olives over sauce. Fold uncovered dough up over filling, letting a strip of filling show in center.

5 Bake in moderate oven (375°) 30 minutes, or until golden. Cut crosswise in thick slices; serve hot.

●

Ham-and-Caraway Foldovers
For these typically Danish open-facers, pile meat and cheese on zesty rye.
Makes 4 servings

3 tablespoons butter or margarine
½ teaspoon prepared mustard
4 slices square rye bread

2 packages (6 ounces each) sliced boiled ham
4 slices caraway cheese (from an 8-ounce package)
   DILLED CUCUMBER CRISPS (recipe follows)

1 Blend butter or margarine with mustard in a cup; spread on bread.

2 Fold ham and cheese slices; pile on top of bread. Garnish with DILLED CUCUMBER CRISPS and a sprig of fresh dill, if you wish.

DILLED CUCUMBER CRISPS—Combine ¼ cup cider vinegar, 2 tablespoons sugar and 1 teaspoon chopped fresh dill in a small bowl; stir until sugar dissolves. Add ½ thinly sliced small cucumber; toss lightly to mix. Chill at least an hour to season.

●

1687

Sun-Glow Salad
Dollop of apricot-pecan cream tops sweet-sour carrot relish on pumpernickel bread.
Makes 4 servings

4 medium-size carrots, pared and grated
1 tablespoon honey
1 tablespoon lemon juice

SANDWICHES—OPEN AND SHUT

½ cup cream for whipping
1 teaspoon sugar
2 tablespoons finely chopped dried apricots
1 tablespoon chopped pecans
4 small slices pumpernickel bread, buttered

1 Place carrots in a medium-size bowl; drizzle honey and lemon juice over; toss to mix well. Chill at least 30 minutes to season.
2 When ready to serve, beat cream with sugar just until it mounds softly in a small bowl; fold in apricots and pecans.
3 Spoon carrot mixture on top of buttered bread slices; top with a fluff of apricot cream and a pecan half, if you wish.

Mediterranean Medley
Men will go for this satisfying stack of shrimps, hard-cooked eggs and macaroni and olive salads on sliced rolls.
Makes 4 servings

4 club rolls, each cut crosswise into 4 slices
⅓ cup bottled garlic salad dressing
   Bibb lettuce
1 container (1 pound) prepared macaroni salad
2 hard-cooked eggs, shelled and sliced
1 small cucumber, pared and sliced
½ cup olive salad (from a 12-ounce jar)
2 cans (5 ounces each) deveined shrimps, drained and rinsed
4 rolled anchovies (from a 2-ounce can)
   Potato chips

1 Place slices from 1 roll on each of 4 serving plates; drizzle with salad dressing; top with lettuce, then macaroni salad, spreading into an even layer to cover rolls.
2 Top macaroni with layers of sliced egg and cucumber, olive salad and shrimps; garnish with an anchovy. Serve with potato chips and additional salad dressing for everyone to sprinkle over top, if you wish.

Denver Sandwich
Makes 4 servings

1 small onion, chopped (¼ cup)
½ green pepper, chopped
3 tablespoons butter or margarine
6 eggs
6 tablespoons milk

Salt and pepper
2 toasted, buttered, split hamburger rolls

1 Sauté onion and green pepper slowly in butter or margarine in medium-size frying pan 5 minutes.
2 Beat eggs slightly with milk and salt and pepper; pour into same pan; scramble with onion-green pepper mixture just until set.
3 Spoon onto hot toasted rolls.

Ham Bounty
Ham slices are rolled around tuna salad and whole green beans, then stacked atop white bread.
Makes 4 servings

2 cans (about 7 ounces each) tuna, drained and flaked
1 cup diced celery
2 hard-cooked eggs, shelled and diced
1 can (4 ounces) pimientos, drained and diced
½ cup coarsely broken walnuts
½ cup mayonnaise or salad dressing
½ teaspoon salt
1 can (1 pound) whole Blue Lake green beans, drained
4 tablespoons bottled oil-and-vinegar salad dressing
4 large oval slices white bread
4 thin slices Bermuda onion
12 long slices boiled ham (from three 5-ounce packages)
   Chicory or curly endive
   Preserved watermelon rind or pickle

1 Combine tuna, celery, eggs, pimientos, walnuts, mayonnaise or salad dressing and salt in a large bowl; toss lightly to mix. Chill at least 30 minutes to season and blend flavors.
2 Place beans in a shallow dish; drizzle with 2 tablespoons of the oil-and-vinegar dressing. Chill at least 30 minutes to season.
3 Just before serving, place each slice of bread on a serving plate; drizzle bread with remaining 2 tablespoons dressing; top with an onion slice.
4 Spoon ½ cup of the tuna salad onto each of 8 slices of ham; roll up, jelly-roll fashion. (Filling will hold rolls together.) Place two rolls on each slice of bread.
5 Drain green beans; roll inside remaining ham slices; place on top of tuna rolls. Garnish plates

with a few sprigs of chicory and several pieces of watermelon rind or pickle.

Soufléed Ham Whoppers
Bake at 350° for 15 minutes. Makes 6 servings

2 packages (6 ounces each) boiled ham
6 slices Vienna bread
3 cups potato salad (from delicatessen or dairy department)
3 eggs, separated
¼ teaspoon salt
¼ cup dairy sour cream

1 Place 1 slice of ham on each slice of bread; top with potato salad, then remaining ham; place in a baking pan.
2 Heat in moderate oven (350°) while making topping.
3 While sandwiches heat, beat egg whites until they stand in firm peaks in a medium-size bowl.
4 Beat egg yolks with salt until thick in a small bowl; stir in sour cream; fold into beaten egg whites. Spoon over sandwiches, dividing evenly.
5 Bake in moderate oven (350°) 15 minutes, or until topping is puffed and golden. Serve hot.

Boston Beanie
New England's favorites—brown bread, baked beans, cranberry sauce and coleslaw—make up this summery supper.
Makes 6 servings

1 can (1 pound) Boston brown bread
1 package (6 ounces) sliced ham-bologna
2 cans (1 pound each) pork and beans in tomato sauce, drained
   Sour pickles, sliced lengthwise
1 can (1 pound) jellied cranberry sauce
1 container (1 pound) prepared coleslaw

1 Cut bread into 12 slices; place 2 slices on each of 6 serving plates.
2 Dice ham-bologna (no need to separate slices); stir into beans in a medium-size bowl. Spoon ½ cup onto each slice of bread; crisscross two pickle strips on top.
3 Cut cranberry sauce into 6 slices; place one on each plate, along with coleslaw.

Tijuana Toasties
Makes 6 servings

6 flat cornmeal cakes (6 to a package)
1 pound ground beef
1 small onion, chopped (¼ cup)
2 tablespoons butter or margarine

2 teaspoons chili powder
1 teaspoon salt
2 cans (1 pound each) barbecue beans
1 cup shredded iceberg lettuce
1 package (4 ounces) shredded Cheddar cheese

1 Split cornmeal cakes with a sharp knife; place, cut sides up, on a cookie sheet.
2 Shape ground beef into a patty in a large frying pan. Cook 5 minutes on each side, then break up into small chunks; push to one side. Add onion and butter or margarine to pan; sauté 3 minutes, or until onion is soft. Stir in chili powder and salt; cook 1 minute. Stir in beans; heat slowly to boiling.
3 Heat corn cakes in broiler 2 to 3 minutes, or just until toasted; place 2 pieces on each of 6 serving plates. Spoon beef mixture on top. Sprinkle lettuce over half and grated cheese over remainder. Serve hot with corn chips, if you wish.

Double Corn Toasties
Packaged flat cornmeal "muffins" are heaped with fruited cottage cheese and meat.
Makes 6 sandwiches

1 cup (8 ounces) cream-style cottage cheese
½ cup mandarin-orange segments (from an 11-ounce can), drained and cut up
6 small leaves Boston lettuce
2 packages (6 to a package) flat cornmeal cakes, toasted and lightly buttered
   OR: 6 English muffins, split and toasted
1 pound sliced cooked tongue

1 Mix cottage cheese and orange segments in a small bowl; spoon into lettuce cups. Place on 6 of the cornmeal cakes or muffin halves on serving plates; sprinkle cheese mixture with nutmeg, if you wish.
2 Fold tongue slices; lay, overlapping, on remaining cornmeal cakes or muffins; place beside cheese-topped "sandwiches" on plates.

1689

Double Salad Jumbo
Zippy seasoned asparagus and carrots and crunchy chicken salad perch on crisp golden waffles.
Makes 6 servings

2 cans (5 or 6 ounces each) boned chicken, diced

SANDWICHES—OPEN AND SHUT

1½ cups diced celery
 1 tablespoon chopped parsley
 ½ teaspoon seasoned salt
 ¼ cup mayonnaise or salad dressing
 1 can (1 pound) sliced carrots, drained
 1 can (about 15 ounces) asparagus spears, drained
 3 tablespoons bottled thin French dressing
12 frozen waffles
    Boston lettuce
    Pretzel sticks

1 Combine chicken with celery, parsley and seasoned salt in a medium-size bowl; fold in mayonnaise or salad dressing. Chill at least 30 minutes to season and blend flavors.
2 Place carrots and asparagus in separate piles in a shallow dish; drizzle French dressing over all. Chill at least 30 minutes to season.
3 Just before serving, toast waffles, following label directions; place 2 on each of 6 serving plates; top each with several leaves of lettuce.
4 Spoon ½ cup chicken salad on one waffle

on each plate; arrange carrots and asparagus in bundles on remaining waffles. Garnish each plate generously with pretzel sticks.

Egg Burgers
Makes 4 servings

 4 English muffins
 ¼ cup mayonnaise or salad dressing
 ½ teaspoon mixed salad herbs
 1 can (12 ounces) pork luncheon meat
 4 tablespoons (½ stick) butter or margarine
 8 eggs
 ¼ cup water
 ½ teaspoon salt
    Dash of pepper
 ½ cup thinly sliced celery
 ¼ cup shredded Cheddar cheese
 2 tablespoons chopped parsley
10 cherry tomatoes, halved

1 Split muffins; toast, following label directions. Blend mayonnaise or salad dressing and salad herbs in a cup; spread on muffins; keep warm.
2 Cut luncheon meat into 16 thin slices; sauté in 2 tablespoons of the butter or margarine until lightly browned in a large frying pan; keep warm.
3 Beat eggs with water just until blended in a large bowl; stir in salt, pepper and celery.
4 Melt remaining 2 tablespoons butter or margarine in a medium-size frying pan; pour in egg mixture. Cook slowly, lifting eggs around edge as they cook to let liquid part flow underneath, just until set but still shiny-moist on top.
5 Place 2 muffin halves on each of 4 serving plates; top with meat, then scrambled eggs. Sprinkle half with shredded cheese and chopped parsley, and garnish remainder with halved cherry tomatoes. Serve hot with horn-shape corn snacks and fruit punch, if you wish.

Surprise Sandwiches
Breakfast favorites—bacon and eggs—make this easy lunch or supper sandwich.
Makes 4 servings

12 slices (about ½ pound) bacon
 4 tablespoons (½ stick) butter or margarine
 ½ teaspoon mixed Italian herbs
 2 hero rolls, split
 6 eggs
 6 tablespoons milk
    Salt and pepper
 1 package frozen asparagus spears, cooked and drained
    OR: 1 can (14 ounces) asparagus spears, heated and drained
 4 slices process cheese, each cut into 4 strips

Too busy to cook or eat? Try sunny Egg Burgers.

1 Lay bacon slices in single layer on broiler rack (or use a wire rack set in a jelly-roll pan); broil, without turning, just until crisp.
2 While bacon cooks, melt 2 tablespoons butter or margarine with herbs in medium-size frying pan; brush mixture on cut sides of rolls, using all; wipe pan with paper towel; melt remaining 2 tablespoons butter or margarine in same pan.
3 Beat eggs with milk in medium-size bowl; season with salt and pepper; pour into heated pan; cook over low heat, stirring gently from bottom and side as eggs begin to set; take pan from heat while eggs are still creamy-soft.
4 Arrange hot asparagus and bacon strips on buttered rolls, dividing evenly; spoon eggs on top; crisscross cheese strips over eggs.
5 Place on broiler rack on pan drained of bacon fat; broil just until cheese is melted; serve hot.

HEROES AND HOBOES

Chicken Cacciatore Surfers
Makes 4 servings

4 chicken breasts, weighing about 12 ounces each
4 tablespoons all-purpose flour
1¼ teaspoons salt
¼ teaspoon pepper
¼ cup vegetable oil
4 large ripe tomatoes, diced
½ cup water
2 tablespoons instant minced onion
2 teaspoons sugar
1 teaspoon dry parsley flakes
½ teaspoon leaf basil, crumbled.
4 hero rolls
1 medium-size green pepper, halved, seeded and diced

1 Skin, bone and halve chicken breasts; slice each half to make 2 thin cutlets.
2 Combine flour, salt and pepper in a paper bag; add chicken, a few pieces at a time and coat well; shake off excess flour.
3 Sauté chicken in vegetable oil in a large frying pan, turning to brown on both sides; set chicken aside and keep warm.
4 Add tomatoes, water, onion, sugar, parsley and basil to same pan; simmer, stirring frequently, about 5 minutes. Place chicken over sauce in a single layer. Simmer, uncovered, about 10 minutes, or until chicken is tender and sauce has thickened.
5 Cut a wedge from top of each roll deep

enough to hold some sauce. Place 4 pieces of chicken and some of the sauce in rolls; spoon remaining sauce over chicken; sprinkle the tops with diced green pepper.

Chicken-Cheese Puff
Bake at 375° for 55 minutes. Makes 4 servings

1 cup milk
4 tablespoons (½ stick) butter or margarine
1 teaspoon onion salt
¼ teaspoon pepper
1 cup sifted all-purpose flour
4 eggs
1 package (6 ounces) sliced Swiss cheese, diced
2 cups diced cooked chicken
1 cup finely chopped celery
½ cup mayonnaise or salad dressing
1 can (4½ ounces) deviled ham
2 tablespoons lemon juice

1 Heat milk, butter or margarine, ½ teaspoon of the onion salt and pepper just to boiling in a medium-size saucepan. Add flour all at once; stir vigorously with a wooden spoon 2 minutes, or until batter forms a thick smooth ball that follows spoon around pan. Remove from heat.
2 Beat in eggs, 1 at a time, until batter is shiny-smooth.
3 Set aside ¼ cup of the diced cheese; stir remainder into mixture in saucepan. Drop batter by heaping tablespoonfuls onto a large cookie sheet to form a rectangle about 12x5. (Batter will spread during baking to make a long loaf.) Sprinkle with the ¼ cup cheese.
4 Bake in moderate oven (375°) 45 minutes, or until puffed and golden.
5 While puff bakes, combine chicken and celery in a large bowl. Blend mayonnaise or salad dressing, deviled ham, lemon juice and remaining ½ teaspoon onion salt in a small bowl; fold into chicken mixture.
6 Cut a thin slice from top of puff; scoop out any bits of soft dough from bottom with a teaspoon. Spoon chicken mixture into bottom; set top back in place.
7 Bake 10 minutes longer, or until filling heats through. Carefully slide onto a large serving platter; cut crosswise into 4 thick slices.

1691

California Biddy Bunwiches
A new version of chicken salad with tangy golden pineapple and crunchy almonds.
Makes 6 servings

SANDWICHES—OPEN AND SHUT

2 whole chicken breasts (about 1½ pounds)
2 cups water
1 medium-size onion, sliced
  Handful of celery tops
1 teaspoon salt (for chicken)
3 peppercorns
1 can (14 ounces) pineapple tidbits, drained
1 cup diced celery
½ cup slivered almonds
½ cup mayonnaise
2 tablespoons milk
¼ teaspoon salt (for salad)
¼ teaspoon dry mustard
⅛ teaspoon pepper
6 Vienna rolls, split and buttered
  Lettuce
  Cherry tomatoes

1 Combine chicken breasts, water, onion, celery tops, 1 teaspoon salt and peppercorns in large saucepan. Simmer, covered, 20 to 30 minutes, or until chicken is tender. Let stand until cool enough to handle, then skin chicken and take meat from bones. Dice chicken (you should have about 2 cups).

2 Combine chicken, pineapple, celery and almonds in medium-size bowl. Mix mayonnaise and pepper in 1-cup measure; stir into chicken mixture, tossing lightly to mix; chill until serving time.

3 Line buttered rolls with lettuce; fill with salad mixture, dividing evenly. Top each with 2 or 3 cherry tomatoes.

Galway Stacks
Makes 4 sandwiches

½ medium-size head of cabbage, trimmed and finely shredded (6 cups)
1 can (4 ounces) red chili peppers, drained and chopped
1 medium-size onion, chopped fine (½ cup)
¼ cup cider vinegar
3 tablespoons vegetable oil
¼ cup sugar
1 teaspoon salt
⅛ teaspoon pepper
4 poppy seed rolls
4 tablespoons (½ stick) butter or margarine

Three handsome summer heroes (left to right): Chicken Cacciatore Surfers, Stuffed Ham Slices, Galway Stacks.

Zeroing in for a close-up of Stuffed Ham Slices.

2 packages (4 ounces each) sliced corned-
beef loaf

1 Place cabbage, chili peppers and onion in a medium-size bowl.
2 Combine vinegar, vegetable oil, sugar, salt and pepper in a cup; stir until sugar dissolves. Pour over cabbage mixture; toss lightly to mix. Let stand, stirring often, at least 1 hour to season; drain well.
3 Split rolls; spread with butter or margarine. Place about ¼ cup of the cabbage mixture on each slice of corned beef; roll up tightly, jelly-roll fashion. Place 3 meat rolls on bottom half of each buttered roll; cover with remaining half.

●

Stroganoff Subs
Makes 4 sandwiches

    1 chuck beefsteak, cut ½ inch thick and
      weighing about 1½ pounds
    3 tablespoons butter or margarine
    2 envelopes instant beef broth
      OR: 2 teaspoons granulated beef bouillon
2½ cups water
    2 tablespoons sliced green onions
    1 can (3 or 4 ounces) sliced mushrooms
    4 hero rolls
    1 tablespoon all-purpose flour
    ½ cup dairy sour cream

1 Trim fat and bone from steak; cut steak into strips about 1 inch wide and 2 inches long. Brown, half at a time, in part of the butter or margarine in a large frying pan.
2 Stir in beef broth, 2 cups of the water, and green onions. Heat to boiling; cover tightly. Simmer 1½ hours, or until beef is tender. Stir in mushrooms and liquid.
3 While meat cooks, cut a thin slice from top of each roll; hollow out insides and set aside with tops to make croutons for another day. Place rolls on a cookie sheet; heat in moderate oven (350°) 10 minutes, or until lightly toasted.
4 Blend flour and remaining ½ cup water until smooth in a cup; stir into meat mixture. Cook, stirring constantly, until mixture thickens and boils 1 minute. *Very slowly* stir in sour cream. (Do not let mixture boil.)
5 Place rolls on serving plates; spoon meat mixture into hollows. Sprinkle with chopped parsley, if you wish. Serve hot.

●

Stuffed Ham Slices
Makes 16 sandwiches

    1 loaf unsliced Italian bread (about 18 inches
      long)

    ¼ cup mayonnaise or salad dressing
    ⅓ cup chopped parsley
    1 package (8 ounces) cream cheese
    ¾ cup very finely chopped celery
    ½ cup shredded Cheddar cheese
    2 tablespoons very finely chopped onion
    ¼ teaspoon salt
    2 packages (4 ounces each) sliced boiled ham
      (8 slices)
    1 large dill pickle

1 Split bread; hollow out each half with a fork, leaving a ½-inch-thick shell. (Save insides to make a crumb topping for a casserole.)
2 Spread mayonnaise or salad dressing over hollows in loaf; sprinkle parsley over mayonnaise.
3 Blend cream cheese, celery, Cheddar cheese, onion and salt in a medium-size bowl; spoon into bread halves, packing down well with back of spoon and leaving a small hollow down center.
4 Quarter pickle lengthwise; roll each quarter inside a double-thick slice of ham. Place rolls, end to end, in center of bottom half of loaf; cover with remaining half of bread. Wrap loaf tightly in transparent wrap; chill several hours.
5 To serve, cut into 16 slices. Garnish with parsley sprigs, if you wish.

1693

●

Stuffed Salad Rolls
A little salad goes far in these inviting summer sandwiches.
Makes 4 servings, 2 rolls each

    2 cups chopped lettuce
    1 cups diced cooked meat, fish or chicken*

½ cup diced process American or Swiss cheese
½ cup chopped celery
½ cup mayonnaise
2 tablespoons pickle relish
¼ teaspoon curry powder
8 frankfurter rolls, split, toasted and buttered

1 Combine lettuce with meat, fish or chicken, cheese and celery in medium-size bowl.
2 Blend mayonnaise, pickle relish and curry powder in small bowl; stir into salad mixture to coat well; pile into prepared rolls.

* You can use ham, tongue, cold cuts, tuna, shrimps or crabmeat.

Cold-Cut Roll-Ups
Roll crisp coleslaw inside cold cuts and pile on big slices of zesty rye.
Makes 6 sandwiches

1 small head cabbage (about 2 pounds)
2 tablespoons sugar
2 tablespoons mayonnaise or salad dressing
2 tablespoons light cream or table cream
2 tablespoons lemon juice
½ teaspoon salt
⅛ teaspoon pepper
½ cup (1 stick) butter or margarine
1 teaspoon prepared mustard
6 large slices rye bread
2 packages (6 ounces each) assorted Italian cold cuts
6 sweet yellow wax peppers

1 Shred cabbage into a large bowl. (There should be about 8 cups.) Sprinkle with sugar; chill at least 30 minutes.
2 Blend mayonnaise or salad dressing, cream and lemon juice in a cup; pour over cabbage. Sprinkle with salt and pepper; toss lightly with two forks to mix.
3 Blend butter or margarine with mustard in a small bowl; spread on bread.
4 Drain coleslaw. Spoon about ¼ cup on each slice of meat; roll up. Pile on bread, dividing evenly. Garnish each with a pepper.

1694

Hawaiian Bologna Buns
Salad-style filling seasoned with soy sauce bakes inside crispy hard rolls.
Bake at 425° for 35 minutes. Makes 4 sandwiches

4 large hard rolls
2 tablespoons butter or margarine

2 tablespoons instant-type flour
1 cup milk
2 teaspoons soy sauce
½ teaspoon curry powder
¼ teaspoon salt
¾ pound bologna, cut in ¼-inch cubes
1 can (about 9 ounces) crushed pineapple, well drained
¼ cup sliced green onions

1 Cut a thin slice across top of each roll and set aside for Step 3. Cut out centers of rolls to make shells. (Save centers to use for a crumb topper or croutons.)
2 Combine butter or margarine, flour and milk in a small saucepan; cook, stirring constantly, until sauce thickens and boils 1 minute; remove from heat. Stir in seasonings.
3 Mix bologna, pineapple and green onions in a medium-size bowl; stir in sauce. Spoon into rolls, dividing evenly; set tops of rolls over filling. Wrap each roll in foil.
4 Bake in hot oven (425°) 35 minutes, or until heated through.

Frankfurter Hoboes
Grated Cheddar melts so invitingly atop hotdogs and creamy macaroni on onion rolls.
Make 6 sandwiches

12 frankfurters (1½ pounds)
2 cans (1 pound each) macaroni and cheese
2 teaspoons dry mustard
6 onion rolls, split and toasted
Prepared sandwich spread
1 package (4 ounces) shredded Cheddar cheese

1 Place frankfurters in a large saucepan of boiling water; cover; remove from heat. Let stand 5 minutes, or until heated through; drain.
2 Mix macaroni and cheese with mustard in a medium-size saucepan; heat slowly just until bubbly.
3 Place toasted rolls, halves together, on a cookie sheet; spread with sandwich spread. Top each with hot macaroni mixture, then 2 frankfurters; sprinkle with cheese.
4 Broil, 4 to 6 inches from heat, 5 minutes, or until cheese melts and bubbles up. Serve hot.

Vienna Heroes
Little sausages and diced potatoes in a sweet-sour dressing make these hot hearties.
Makes 6 servings, 2 rolls each

3 cups diced pared raw potatoes (about 3 medium-size)

Open-face sandwiches that put on a pretty party face: Cold Cut Roll-Ups. To accompany: Tall, cool lemonade.

1 teaspoon salt (for potatoes)
1 cup water
2 cups diced celery
1 small onion, chopped (¼ cup)
½ cup diced dill pickle
3 cans (about 4 ounces each) Vienna sausages, cut into ¼-inch slices
2 tablespoons butter or margarine
2 tablespoons brown sugar
2 tablespoons cider vinegar
2 tablespoons water
½ teaspoon salt (for salad)
¼ teaspoon pepper
12 frankfurter rolls, toasted and buttered

1 Cook potatoes with 1 teaspoon salt and water in medium-size saucepan 15 minutes, or until tender; drain. Mix in celery, onion and dill pickle
2 Sauté sausages, stirring often, in butter or margarine until lightly browned in medium-size frying pan. Stir in brown sugar, vinegar, water, ½ teaspoon salt and pepper; heat to boiling; pour over potato mixture; toss to mix well.

3 Mound salad mixture onto rolls, dividing evenly; serve hot.

●

Super Subs
Luncheon meat, eggs and cheese, along with peppy extras, make the salad filling.
Makes 6 servings

3 hard-cooked eggs, diced
½ can (12 ounces) pork luncheon meat, diced
1 package (8 ounces) process American cheese, diced
2 tablespoons mayonnaise
2 tablespoons pickle relish
1 teaspoon prepared mustard
6 frankfurter rolls, buttered
  Lettuce
  Stuffed green olives
  Radishes

1 Combine eggs, pork luncheon meat, cheese, mayonnaise, pickle relish and mustard in me-

1695

dium-size bowl; toss lightly to mix. (If made ahead, chill until serving time.)

2 Line buttered rolls with lettuce; fill with salad mixture, dividing evenly. Garnish with stuffed green olives and radishes threaded onto wooden picks, kebab style.

Supper Sandwich
Bake at 400° for 45 minutes. Makes 6 servings

1 loaf Vienna bread, plain or with sesame seeds
  Melted butter or margarine
1 can (12 ounces) pork luncheon meat
1 package (½ pound) process Swiss cheese, grated
¾ cup mayonnaise or salad dressing
¼ cup sweet-pickle relish
1 tablespoon prepared mustard
1 teaspoon cider vinegar

1 Cut loaf into ¾-inch-wide slices almost through to bottom; brush cut sides with butter or margarine.

2 Mash meat with fork in large bowl; blend in remaining ingredients.

3 Spread meat mixture generously between slices (if bread is plain, brush top with melted butter or margarine and sprinkle with sesame seeds, if you wish); wrap loosely in aluminum foil; place on cookie sheet.

4 Bake in hot oven (400°) about 45 minutes, or until heated through.

Italian-Sausage Heroes
Plump sausages perch atop herb-seasoned vegetables in crisp rolls.
Bake at 350° for 10 minutes. Makes 4 sandwiches

8 sweet Italian sausages (about 1¼ pounds)
1 Bermuda onion, peeled and chopped
2 large green peppers, quartered, seeded and sliced
1 teaspoon salt
1 teaspoon sugar
1 teaspoon Italian seasoning
2 large tomatoes, chopped
2 large hero rolls
  Butter or margarine

1696

1 Score sausages every ½ inch; sauté slowly in a large frying pan 15 minutes, or until cooked through; drain on paper toweling.

The best of Italy goes into Italian-Sausage Heroes.

2 Pour off all drippings, then measure 3 tablespoons and return to pan; stir in onion and sauté until soft. Stir in peppers, salt, sugar and Italian seasoning; cover; cook 5 minutes.

3 Stir in tomatoes; place sausages on top; cover. Steam 5 minutes, or until mixture is bubbly-hot.

4 While vegetables cook, split hero rolls; cut out center of each half to make a boat-shape shell. (Save centers to use for a crumb topper or croutons.) Spread insides of rolls with butter or margarine; place on a cookie sheet.

5 Heat in moderate oven (350°) 10 minutes or until crispy-hot. Place on serving plates; spoon vegetable mixture into hollows; top each with 2 sausages. Garnish with a quartered stalk of Belgian endive and a radish posy, if you wish. To fix, trim radish, then cut lengthwise into twelfths from root end almost to stem end. Chill in a bowl of ice and water.

Ship-a-Heroes
Big rolls filled with creamy egg salad and rigged with cold-cut "sails" make a fun meal for juniors.
Makes 4 servings

4 hero rolls
4 tablespoons olive oil or vegetable oil
2 tablespoons wine vinegar or cider vinegar
2 teaspoons sugar
½ teaspoon salt
  Romaine
  CREAMY EGG SALAD (recipe follows)
1 package (6 or 8 ounces) sliced bologna
1 package (6 or 8 ounces) sliced salami
1 small green pepper, halved, seeded and cut
  in 1-inch squares

1 Slice off top of each roll; cut out middle of roll with a sharp knife to make a boat-shape shell. (Save tops and middle pieces to make croutons.)
2 Mix oil, vinegar, sugar and salt in a cup; brush over insides of rolls.
3 Line each roll with romaine; fill with CREAMY EGG SALAD. (It will take about ⅔ cup for each.)
4 To make sails, thread bologna and salami slices with green-pepper pieces onto long wooden picks, stick into tops of sandwiches. Garnish with anchovy fillets, rolled up.
  CREAMY EGG SALAD—Combine 8 hard-cooked eggs, shelled and chopped; ½ cup finely chopped celery; ¼ cup finely chopped green

pepper; 8 anchovy fillets (from a 2-ounce can), chopped; and ½ cup mayonnaise or salad dressing in a small bowl; stir lightly to mix. Makes about 2⅔ cups.

●

Whopper Heroes
Pile meat, cheese, egg and tomato slices on split French bread, then let everyone cut off a "sandwich."
Makes 6 to 9 servings

Split 3 loaves of French bread in half; spread generously with a mixture of ¾ cup mayonnaise or salad dressing and 3 tablespoons prepared mustard. Cover bottom halves of bread with lettuce; place folded slices of spiced ham, Swiss cheese, liverwurst, salami, process American cheese, corned beef and boiled ham on top. (Or choose your own favorite cold cuts and cheeses.) Tuck slices of hard-cooked egg, tomato, onion and red and green pepper between meats; drizzle lightly with olive oil for a real Italian touch. The sandwich can have a garnish of pickled yellow wax peppers and pickled sweet red peppers threaded onto long wooden picks, kebab style, and a bow of red- and green-

Whopper Heroes are the heroes to end all heroes—one unbelievable line-up. It's a help-yourself sandwich.

pepper strips. To serve, set kebabs aside; cover filling with spread top of bread; cut in half or thirds crosswise.

Liver-and-Egg Boats

Sliced cucumber and liverwurst, and egg salad make the double fillings for hotdog rolls.
Makes 4 sandwiches

4 hard-cooked eggs, shelled
½ cup mayonnaise or salad dressing
¼ cup chopped parsley
   Salt and pepper
4 split frankfurter rolls
4 leaves romaine
8 slices liverwurst (about ½ pound)
½ medium-size cucumber, pared and cut in 16 slices

1698

1 Press eggs through a sieve or mash with a fork in a small bowl; blend in ¼ cup of the mayonnaise or salad dressing, chopped parsley and salt and pepper to taste.
2 Spread frankfurter rolls with remaining ¼ cup mayonnaise or salad dressing; top half of each with a romaine leaf, then egg salad.
3 Arrange liverwurst and cucumber slices, alternately, on remaining halves of rolls. Sprinkle egg salad with paprika and garnish liverwurst with parsley, if you wish.

Liver-and-Bacon Boats

Makes 6 sandwiches

1 pound chicken livers
⅓ cup unsifted all-purpose flour
3 tablespoons butter or margarine
½ cup dry white wine
½ pound sliced bacon
6 frankfurter rolls
1 tablespoon finely chopped parsley

1 Dip chicken livers in flour in a pie plate; tap off any excess.
2 Brown in butter or margarine in a large frying pan over medium heat; stir in wine. Heat to boiling; cover. Simmer 10 minutes.
3 While livers cook, sauté bacon until crisp in a second large frying pan; remove and drain on paper toweling; keep warm.
4 Heat or toast rolls, then butter, if you wish; place on serving plates. Spoon liver mixture into rolls; sprinkle with parsley; place bacon slices on top.

All-American Hero

Potato salad, sardines, tomatoes and pickles go into this whopper of a sandwich.
Makes 6 servings

2 cups diced, peeled, cooked potatoes
¾ cup chopped celery
1 small onion, chopped (¼ cup)
¼ pound (half an 8-ounce package) process American cheese, cut into small cubes

2 hard-cooked eggs, shelled and chopped
1 teaspoon salt
¼ teaspoon pepper
½ cup mayonnaise
1 teaspoon prepared mustard
1 long loaf French bread, split lengthwise and buttered
2 cans (about 4 ounces each) sardines, drained
2 dill pickles, sliced thin lengthwise
1 tomato, sliced thin

1 Combine potatoes, celery, onion, cheese, eggs, salt and pepper in medium-size bowl; fold in mayonnaise and mustard until well blended.
2 Pile potato salad on bottom half of buttered bread; arrange sardines and pickle and tomato slices in layers on top; replace top crust. Slice crosswise into 6 servings

East-West Tuna Whoppers
Makes 4 sandwiches

1 package (7 ounces) frozen Chinese pea pods
1 can (1 pound) chop suey vegetables
3 tablespoons cornstarch
¾ teaspoon ground ginger
1 tablespoon soy sauce
2 tablespoons butter or margarine
4 sesame-seed buns, split and toasted
2 cans tuna (about 7 ounces each), drained and broken into small chunks
1 bunch green onions, trimmed and sliced (about ⅓ cup)

1 Cook pea pods, following label directions; drain liquid into a 2-cup measure. Drain liquid from vegetables into same measure; add water, if needed, to make 1½ cups.
2 Mix cornstarch and ginger in a medium-size saucepan; stir in the 1½ cups vegetable liquid and soy sauce until smooth. Cook, stirring constantly, until sauce thickens and boils 3 minutes.
3 Stir in pea pods, vegetables and butter or margarine; heat slowly to boiling.
4 Place buns, cut sides up, on serving plates; spoon part of the sauce mixture over buns; top with tuna, then remaining sauce. Sprinkle sliced green onions over all. Serve immediately and accompany with knife and fork.

Western Tuna Buns
Makes 8 sandwiches

1 can (about 7 ounces) tuna, drained and flaked
1 can (about 9 ounces) pineapple tidbits, well drained

½ cup finely diced celery
¼ cup finely diced green pepper
¼ cup toasted slivered almonds
¼ cup mayonnaise or salad dressing
½ teaspoon salt
⅛ teaspoon pepper
1 teaspoon lemon juice
8 hamburger rolls, split, toasted and buttered
    Romaine or Boston lettuce

1 Combine tuna, pineapple, celery, green pepper, almonds, mayonnaise or salad dressing, salt, pepper and lemon juice in bowl; mix lightly.
2 Line hamburger rolls with romaine or lettuce; fill with salad mixture; wrap each in a paper napkin for easy eating.

Oven Tuna Buns
Bake at 350° for 25 minutes. Makes 4 servings

2 cans (about 7 ounces each) tuna, drained and flaked
1 package (3 or 4 ounces) cream cheese, cut in small cubes
6 water chestnuts, drained and chopped
2 tablespoons finely cut chives
2 tablespoons chopped parsley
⅓ cup mayonnaise or salad dressing
2 tablespoons chili sauce
4 large poppy-seed rolls

1 Combine tuna, cream cheese, water chestnuts, chives and parsley in a medium-size bowl.
2 Blend mayonnaise or salad dressing and chili sauce in a cup; fold into tuna mixture.
3 Cut a thin slice from top of each roll; hollow out inside, leaving a ¼-inch-thick shell. Spoon tuna mixture into hollows, dividing evenly; set tops of rolls back in place. Wrap each sandwich in foil; place on a cookie sheet.
4 Bake in moderate oven (350°) 25 minutes. Unwrap; serve hot.

1699

Oyster Pacesetters
Makes 6 servings

6 medium-size tomatoes
½ cup bottled French dressing
12 club rolls
½ cup (1 stick) butter or margarine, melted
½ cup unsifted all-purpose flour
1 cup fine dry bread crumbs
2 eggs

Crab isn't the usual sandwich filling, but Alaska king crab and frozen peas, Swiss cheese, celery, parsley and mayonnaise team for Hot Crab Salad Boats.

1700

2 cans (8 ounces each) oysters, drained
Shortening or vegetable oil for frying
2 cups shredded iceberg lettuce

1 Peel tomatoes; cut each in 6 wedges; place in a shallow dish. Drizzle French dressing over top; let stand at least 15 minutes to season.
2 Cut a thin slice from top of each roll; hollow out inside, leaving a ¼-inch-thick shell. Brush rolls all over with melted butter or margarine; place on a large cookie sheet.
3 Heat in hot oven (400°) 10 minutes, or until hot.
4 Place flour and bread crumbs on separate sheets of wax paper; beat eggs slightly in a pie plate. Dip oysters in flour, then in beaten egg and bread crumbs to coat well.

5 Melt enough shortening or pour vegetable oil into a large frying pan to fill two thirds full; heat to 375°. Drop oysters into hot shortening; fry 2 to 3 minutes, or until golden. Remove with a slotted spoon and drain on paper toweling.
6 Place 2 rolls on each of 6 serving plates; pile oysters into 6 rolls. Place lettuce in remaining rolls; overlap tomato wedges on top, then drizzle dressing from dish over lettuce.

Curried Fish Boat
Makes 6 to 8 servings

1 large loaf French bread
2 packages frozen fish sticks (8 to 12 to a package)

2 tablespoons butter or margarine
2 tablespoons all-purpose flour
1 teaspoon salt
½ teaspoon curry powder
2 cups milk
4 hard-cooked eggs, shelled and chopped coarsely

1 Hollow out bread with a sharp knife to make a boat-shape shell about 1½ inches thick. (Set trimmings aside to use for croutons or a crumb topper.)
2 Quarter frozen fish sticks; heat, following label directions.
3 Melt butter or margarine in a medium-size saucepan; stir in flour, salt and curry powder. Cook, stirring constantly, just until bubbly. Stir in milk; continue cooking and stirring until sauce thickens and boils 1 minute; fold in eggs.
4 Pile fish into bread boat; spoon some of the hot egg sauce over top; pass remaining separately. To serve, slice loaf crosswise. Serve hot.

Hot Crab Salad Boats

Rolls are buttery-crisp; filling is refreshing and just hearty enough for summer eating.
Bake at 400° for 15 minutes. Makes 6 servings

2 packages (about 6 ounces each) frozen Alaska king crabmeat, thawed and drained
1 cup chopped celery
1 cup frozen green peas
¼ pound (half an 8-ounce package) process Swiss cheese, cut into small cubes
¼ cup chopped parsley
¾ cup mayonnaise
6 long hero rolls
4 tablespoons (½ stick) butter or margarine, melted

1 Cut crabmeat into bite-size pieces, carefully removing any thin bony tissue. Combine with celery, peas, cheese and parsley in medium-size bowl; mix in mayonnaise.
2 Cut off a slice across top of each roll; cut out middle with a sharp knife to make a boat-shape shell. (Save tops and middle pieces to make toasty croutons.) Brush inside of shells with melted butter or margarine; fill with crabmeat mixture. Wrap each separately in foil.
3 Bake in hot oven (400°) 15 minutes, or just until filling is hot. Thread a lemon wedge and 2 ripe olives onto a wooden pick to serve with each sandwich, if you wish.

DAINTY PARTY SANDWICHES

GIVE FLAVOR AND FLAIR TO PARTY SANDWICHES

Good Insurance—Removing delicate tart shells from muffin cups without breaking is easy if you first line cups with foil. Smooth foil as well as you can so it will peel off neatly.

Fun Fancies—For sandwich-making magic, start with bread of contrasting colors and mark each slice in triangles. Cut the same design in each, lift out with knife tip; switch trims.

1701

Conversation Pieces—Flower holder helps perky vegetable posies keep their heads high. To fix them, cut blossoms from thin carrot slices and green pepper; fasten onto slender stalks of celery with short wooden picks.

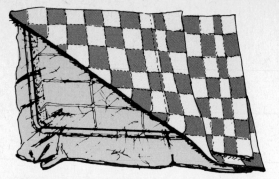

Storing Tip—Depend on your refrigerator to hold make-ahead dainties appetizingly fresh and moist until serving time. Place them in a shallow pan lined with damp paper toweling and transparent wrap; cover and keep chilled.

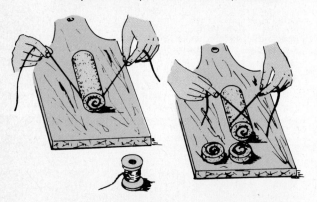

Clean Cut—A long thread makes a nifty slicer for pinwheel sandwiches and helps to keep the soft dough in trim rounds. Just place the thread around the roll, crisscross the two ends over top, and pull gently but tightly.

1702

Smashing Success—To roll bread without cracking, follow these how-tos: Trim the crusts from fresh soft bread and flatten each slice. Work with only a few slices at a time to prevent the bread from drying out.

Ribbon Sandwich Cake
Makes 16 servings

1 round loaf unsliced white bread
2 tablespoons butter or margarine
2 cans (about 5 ounces each) chicken spread
1 can or jar (4 ounces) pimientos, drained and chopped
1 small firm ripe avocado
1 teaspoon lemon juice
2 packages (8 ounces each) cream cheese
2 tablespoons mayonnaise or salad dressing
2 tablespoons milk
½ cup chopped parsley

1 Cut a thin slice from bread to make top flat; set aside to use for croutons or a crumb topper. Slice bottom section crosswise into 4 even layers; spread 3 of the layers with butter or margarine.
2 Mix chicken spread and pimientos in a small bowl; spread evenly on 2 of the layers.
3 Halve avocado; pit, peel and cut into small chunks; place in a small bowl. Sprinkle with lemon juice, then mash with a fork. Blend in 1 package of the cream cheese and mayonnaise or salad dressing; spread on one of the remaining layers.
4 Stack the 3 layers, with avocado layer between, on a large serving plate; place plain layer on top.
5 Beat remaining package of cream cheese with milk until fluffy-smooth in a small bowl; spread over side and top of loaf. Press parsley firmly onto side. Chill. Just before serving, garnish with a cluster of radish roses, if you wish. Cut into wedges with a sharp knife.
Hostess Note: Loaf may be made and frosted three to four hours ahead. It slices best if thoroughly chilled first.

Mushroom-Butter Rounds
Makes 32 small sandwiches

¾ cup (1½ sticks) butter or margarine
¾ cup chopped watercress
¼ teaspoon salt
16 slices cracked-wheat bread (about 1 one-pound loaf)
8 medium-size mushrooms, sliced lengthwise
2 tablespoons lemon juice
1 can or jar (4 ounces) whole pimientos, drained

1 Blend butter or margarine, watercress, and salt in a small bowl.
2 Cut 2 rounds from each slice of bread with a 1½-inch cutter to make 32 in all; spread with watercress butter. Brush mushroom slices with

lemon juice to keep them white; place one on each buttered bread round.

3 Slit pimientos down side and open out flat, then cut out tiny leaf shapes with a truffle cutter; place 2 around mushroom stems on bread rounds.

Hostess Note: Watercress butter may be spread on bread at least an hour ahead. Place sandwiches in a single layer on a cookie sheet or tray, cover tightly to prevent drying, and chill. Cut pimiento leaves ahead and chill, ready to place on sandwiches at serving time. Slice mushrooms just before serving, as they tend to darken on standing.

Pagoda Ham Cups

Bake cups at 400° for 5 minutes. Makes 32 tiny tarts

```
 8  slices cheese bread
 2  tablespoons butter or margarine, softened
 1  envelope unflavored gelatin
 2  tablespoons sugar
 ¼  teaspoon salt
 1  cup water
 2  tablespoons lemon juice
 2  tablespoons sweet-pickle relish
 2  long slices boiled ham
    Chicory or curly endive
```

1 Trim crusts from bread; roll each slice thin with a rolling pin. Spread with butter or margarine; cut into quarters. Press each quarter, buttered side down, in a tiny muffin-pan cup.

2 Bake in hot oven (400°) 5 minutes, or until lightly toasted. Remove from pans; cool on wire racks.

3 Mix gelatin, sugar and salt in a small saucepan; stir in water. Heat slowly, stirring constantly, until gelatin dissolves; remove from heat. Stir in lemon juice. Chill until as thick as unbeaten egg white.

4 Fold in pickle relish; pour into a loaf pan, 8x4x2. Chill until firm. (Overnight is best.)

5 Cut gelatin mixture into 32 squares; place one in each bread cup. Cut each slice of ham into 16 strips; roll each, jelly-roll fashion; fasten with a wooden pick. Thread a snip of chicory onto bottom of pick; stick one into gelatin in each cup.

Hostess Note: Fix bread cups a day or two ahead, if you wish; store in a loosely covered container. Before filling, recrisp in moderate oven (350°) 2 minutes. Make gelatin mixture a day ahead so it will be firmly set, but wait to put into bread cups until an hour before serving.

Ham Pinwheels

Peppy parsley-flecked meat filling twirls inside dainty quick-fix rolls.

Bake at 375° for 15 minutes. Makes about 5 dozen

```
 2  cans (4½ ounces each) deviled ham
 1  can (3 or 4 ounces) chopped mushrooms,
    drained and minced
 ¼  cup minced dill pickle
 2  tablespoons chopped parsley
 1  tablespoon prepared mustard
 2  packages refrigerated crescent dinner rolls
```

1 Blend deviled ham, mushrooms, dill pickle, parsley and mustard in a small bowl.

2 Separate 1 package of the rolls into 4 rectangles; pinch dough at markings to seal. Spread each rectangle with 3 tablespoons of the ham mixture; starting at short end, roll up; pinch dough again to seal. Cut each roll into 8 even slices. Place on a large cookie sheet. Repeat with remaining package of rolls and ham filling.

3 Bake in moderate oven (375°) 15 minutes, or until golden. Serve hot or cold.

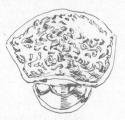

Deviled Ham Leaves

Makes 32 small sandwiches

```
32  slices soft white bread (about 2 one-pound
    loaves)
 2  cans (4½ ounces each) deviled ham
 3  cartons (4 ounces each) whipped cream
    cheese
    Green food coloring
```

1 Cut two leaf shapes from each slice of bread with a 1½-inch-long cookie cutter.

2 Blend deviled ham and 2 cartons of the cream cheese until smooth in a medium-size bowl; spread on bread cutouts to make 32 sandwiches.

3 Blend remaining carton of cream cheese with a few drops food coloring to tint pale green in a small bowl.

4 Fit a plain tip onto a cake-decorating set; fill with cheese mixture. Press out onto tops of sandwiches to resemble markings on leaves.

Hostess Note: Sandwiches may be made up and decorated about an hour ahead. Place in a

1703

single layer on a cookie sheet or tray, cover tightly to keep them from drying out, and chill until serving time.

●

Buffet Chicken-Sandwich Basket

It will be the talk of your party! Homemade bread is sliced and made into sandwiches, then arranged in the shell of the loaf.
Bake at 350° for 50 minutes. Makes 4 dozen small sandwiches

    ½ cup milk
    3 tablespoons sugar
    1½ teaspoons salt
    ½ cup (1 stick) butter or margarine
    2 envelopes active dry yeast
    ½ cup very warm water
    2 eggs, well beaten
    4 cups sifted all-purpose flour
    Sesame seeds
    PARTY CHICKEN SALAD (recipe follows)

1 Scald milk with sugar, salt and butter or margarine in a small saucepan; cool to lukewarm.
2 Sprinkle yeast into very warm water in a large bowl. ("Very warm" water should feel comfortably warm when dropped on wrist.) Stir until yeast dissolves, then stir in cooled milk mixture and beaten eggs.
3 Beat in 2 cups of the flour until smooth. Stir in remaining flour until well blended, then beat vigorously with a spoon, scraping down side of bowl often, 100 strokes, or until dough is shiny-elastic.
4 Coat top lightly with soft butter or margarine. Cover with a clean towel; let rise in a warm place, away from draft, 1 hour, or until double in bulk.
5 Stir dough down; let rise again 30 minutes, or until double in bulk. Stir dough down again; beat another 100 strokes.
6 Grease an 8-inch spring-form pan; sprinkle bottom and side with sesame seeds; spoon dough into pan; sprinkle with sesame seeds. Cover; let rise again, 30 minutes, or until *not quite* double in bulk.
7 Bake in moderate oven (350°) 50 minutes, or until bread gives a hollow sound when tapped. Remove from pan; cool completely on

1704

A cake and platter of fancy French pastries? Not at all. They're all party sandwiches: Ribbon Sandwich Cake standing alone, and artfully arrayed on the platter: Mushroom-Butter Rounds, Pagoda Ham Cups, Miniature Salmon Eclairs, Deviled Ham Leaves, Black-Eyed Susans, Strawberry Cornucopias and Orange Cream Crescents. They prove just how beautiful sandwiches are.

a wire rack. Wrap and store. (Bread slices best if made a day ahead.)

8 When ready to make sandwiches, cut a thick slice from top and bottom of loaf with a sharp, long-blade knife and set aside for Steps 10 and 11. Using an up-and-down sawing motion, cut around inside crust to loosen bread in one large round; lift off shell and set aside for Step 10.

9 Slice bread into 8 thin rounds, keeping slices in order. Put each two rounds together with PARTY CHICKEN SALAD; cut each round, spoke fashion, into 12 triangular sandwiches.

10 Place bottom crust and shell of loaf from Step 8 on a large serving plate; arrange the three large rounds of sandwiches in shell. Place remaining sandwiches around edge. Cover all with a damp towel; chill.

11 When ready to serve, set top of loaf in place. Garnish with sprigs of parsley and pitted ripe olives rolled inside carrot curls and threaded onto wooden picks, if you wish. (To make carrot curls, shave a large scraped carrot into long thin strips with a vegetable parer. Roll strips around finger; hold in place with a wooden pick; chill in ice and water until curled.)

Party Chicken Salad
Diced tongue and chopped celery add colorful flecks of red and green.
Makes 3 cups

   1 broiler-fryer (about 2 pounds)
   1 small onion, sliced
     Few celery tops
1½ teaspoons salt
 ⅛ teaspoon pepper
   2 cups water
   1 can (6 ounces) tongue, finely diced (1 cup)
   1 cup chopped celery
   1 cup mayonnaise or salad dressing

1 Simmer chicken, covered, with onion, celery tops, 1 teaspoon of the salt, pepper and water in a large saucepan 45 minutes, or until chicken is tender. (Remaining salt is for salad in Step 3.)

2 Remove chicken from broth; cool until easy to handle. (Chill broth to use for soup another day.) Pull skin from chicken and take meat from bones; dice meat fine.

3 Combine with tongue, celery, mayonnaise or salad dressing and remaining ½ teaspoon salt in a medium-size bowl; toss to mix well. Chill.

Lobster Top Hats
Tiny cherry tomato cups heaped with seafood salad perch atop cucumber sandwiches.
Makes 3 dozen small sandwiches

   1 can (about 6 ounces) lobster meat, drained, boned and finely chopped
  ¼ cup mayonnaise or salad dressing
   1 tablespoon chili sauce
   2 small cucumbers, pared
   9 thin slices square rye bread
   9 thin slices square pumpernickel bread
   6 tablespoons (¾ stick) butter or margarine
 18 cherry tomatoes

1 Mix lobster, mayonnaise or salad dressing and chili sauce in a small bowl. Cut each cucumber into 36 thin slices.

2 Cut 4 rounds from each slice of rye and pumpernickel bread with a 1½-inch cookie cutter; spread each with butter or margarine, then top with a cucumber slice. Stack one each rye and pumpernickel rounds, cucumber side up, to make a double-layer sandwich; repeat with remaining rounds; place on a tray. Cover with a damp towel; chill.

3 Stem tomatoes, then halve crosswise; scoop out pulp with the quarter teaspoon of a measuring-spoon set. Fill each half with lobster mixture; place in a single layer on a tray or large plate; cover; chill.

4 When ready to serve, stand a tomato-lobster cup on each cucumber sandwich, holding in place with a wooden pick, if needed. Garnish with parsley, if you wish. Arrange on serving tray.

Miniature Salmon Éclairs
Bake shells at 400° for 25 minutes. Makes 32 little puffs

 ½ cup water
 4 tablespoons (½ stick) butter or margarine
 ½ cup sifted all-purpose flour
 ⅛ teaspoon salt
 2 eggs
   SALMON SALAD (recipe follows)
   Tiny pickled onions
   Watercress

1 Heat water and butter or margarine to boiling in a medium-size saucepan. Add flour and salt all at once; stir vigorously with a wooden spoon 2 minutes, or until batter forms a thick smooth ball that follows spoon around pan; remove from heat.

2 Beat in eggs, 1 at a time, until batter is shiny-smooth. Divide in half; place each half on a sheet of wax paper.

3 Butter hands; shape batter into logs, 8 inches long and 1½ inches in diameter. Cut each into 16 pieces with a buttered sharp knife. Place, 1 inch apart, on ungreased cookie sheets.

More pretty party sandwiches: Buffet Chicken-Sandwich Basket (left), Lobster Top Hats and Ribbon Rosies (top tier) and Date-Nut Triangles and Pimiento-Cress Whirligigs (bottom). Deliciously showy!

4 Bake in hot oven (400°) 25 minutes, or until puffed and lightly golden. Remove at once from cookie sheets to wire racks; cool completely.
5 Cut a thin slice from top of each éclair with a sharp knife; scoop out any bits of soft dough from bottoms. Fill bottoms with SALMON SALAD; replace tops. Garnish each with a pickled onion and watercress threaded onto a wooden pick.
   SALMON SALAD—Drain liquid from 1 can (about 7 ounces) salmon; flake in a medium-size bowl.

Fold in 1 cup finely diced unpared zucchini, ¼ teaspoon salt, ⅓ cup mayonnaise or salad dressing and 2 teaspoons lemon juice. Makes about 1½ cups.
Hostess Note: Bake éclairs a day or two ahead, if you wish, and store in a loosely covered container. Before filling, recrisp in hot oven (400°) 2 minutes. Filling, too, may be made several hours ahead, then drained and put into shells about an hour before serving.

SANDWICHES—OPEN AND SHUT

Ribbon Rosies

How colorful they look with layers of white and whole-wheat breads striped with ham and cheese fillings.

Makes 3 dozen small sandwiches

6 thin slices white bread
6 thin slices whole-wheat bread
6 tablespoons (¾ stick) butter or margarine
   DEVILED HAM FILLING (recipe follows)
   PARSLEY-CHEESE FILLING (recipe follows)

1 Arrange bread in 3 rows of 4 slices each on a large cutting board, making first and third rows white and second and fourth rows whole wheat. Spread all with butter or margarine.
2 Spread DEVILED HAM FILLING on first and third rows and PARSLEY-CHEESE FILLING on second row; leave fourth row plain.
3 Place each plain slice, buttered side down, on ham-spread slice, then stack on cheese-spread slice, then on another ham-spread slice to make three 4-layer sandwiches. Wrap each in wax paper, foil or transparent wrap; chill at least 2 hours, or overnight.
4 When ready to serve, trim crusts from sandwiches. (Use trimmings for nibbles.) Cut each sandwich into quarters, then cut each quarter into 3 thin slices. Arrange on serving tray.
   DEVILED HAM FILLING—Mix 1 can (4½ ounces) deviled ham, ¼ cup finely chopped celery, 2 tablespoons mayonnaise or salad dressing and 2 teaspoons prepared mustard in a small bowl. Makes ¾ cup.
   PARSLEY-CHEESE FILLING—Combine ¼ cup blue-cheese spread (from a 5-ounce jar), ¼ cup finely chopped radishes and ¼ cup finely chopped parsley in a small bowl. Makes about ⅓ cup.

Pimiento-Cress Whirligigs

Recipe tells how to turn regular sliced white bread into these double-filled fancies.

Makes 30 small sandwiches

½ cup (1 stick) butter or margarine
¼ cup chopped watercress leaves
1 jar (5 ounces) pimiento-cheese spread
   Few drops liquid red pepper seasoning
12 slices soft white bread

1 Cream butter or margarine in a small bowl; stir in watercress. Blend cheese spread and liquid red pepper seasoning in a second small bowl.
2 Trim crusts from bread. Line up 2 slices, slightly overlapping, on a bread board; roll thin with a rolling pin. (Slices will stick together to make a rectangle.) Spread with ⅓ of the watercress butter.
3 Roll 2 more slices of bread; spread with ⅓ of the cheese spread. Place cheese-topped slice on watercress-topped slice, leaving about ½ inch uncovered on one end; starting here, roll up, jelly-roll fashion. (This makes a neatly shaped pinwheel.)
4 Repeat with remaining bread and fillings to make 2 more rolls. Wrap each tightly in wax paper, foil or transparent wrap. Chill at least 2 hours, or overnight.
5 When ready to serve, unwrap rolls; slice each crosswise into 10 pinwheels.

●

Black-Eyed Susans

Makes 32 small sandwiches

1½ dozen hard-cooked eggs
¾ cup mayonnaise or salad dressing
1½ teaspoons prepared mustard
64 slices whole-wheat bread (about 4 one-pound loaves)
   Pitted ripe olives, sliced

1 Shell eggs; cut in half; scoop out yolks. Press yolks through a fine sieve into a medium-size bowl. Save whites to dice and cream for a family meal. Blend mayonnaise or salad dressing and mustard into yolks.
2 Cut 64 flower shapes from bread with a 2½-inch cookie cutter.
3 Measure ½ cup of the yolk mixture and set aside for garnish. Spread remainder on bread cutouts to make 32 sandwiches. Top each with a dot of saved yolk mixture; frame with a ring of olive slices.
Hostess Note: Sandwiches may be made and decorated about an hour ahead. Place in a single layer on a cookie sheet or tray, cover tightly to keep them from drying out and chill until serving time.

●

Asparagus Rolls

Tucked inside each cheese sandwich is a bright asparagus spear.

Makes about 4 dozen small sandwiches

2 bunches fresh asparagus (about 4 pounds)
   Bottled thin French dressing
3 jars (5 ounces each) sharp Cheddar cheese spread
6 tablespoons (¾ stick) butter or margarine
48 slices soft white bread (from 3 loaves)

1 Break tough woody ends from asparagus;

wash stalks well. If scales are large or sandy, cut off with a sharp knife, then wash stalks again. Cut off flowery tip of each stalk to a 3-inch length to use for sandwiches, then chill remaining to cook for a family meal.

2 Tie stalks in two or three bundles; stand upright in a deep large saucepån. Pour in boiling water to depth of about an inch; cover.

3 Cook 15 minutes, or just until crisply tender. Lift out bundles; drain; snip off strings. Place asparagus in a large shallow dish; brush with French dressing; chill several hours to season.

4 Combine cheese spread and butter or margarine in a medium-size bowl; beat until smooth.

5 Trim crusts from bread; roll each slice thin with a rolling pin; spread with cheese mixture. Place a seasoned asparagus spear at one end of each slice; roll up tightly, jelly-roll fashion. Wrap and chill.

Hostess Note: If you prefer to use frozen asparagus spears, you will need about three boxes (10 ounces each). Cook and drain, following label directions, then season, following Step 3 above.

Watercress Whirls
Makes 2 dozen small sandwiches

12 thin slices soft white bread
 6 tablespoons softened butter or margarine
 1 bunch watercress

1 Spread bread smoothly with butter or margarine; cut off crusts; halve each slice diagonally; roll up.

2 Place, rolled side down and close together, in shallow pan lined with wax paper; cover with foil, or with wax paper and a damp clean towel; chill.

3 Wash and dry watercress; snip tops into 1-inch-long sprigs; wrap loosely; chill.

4 To serve, stick a watercress sprig in open end of each roll; arrange on tray.

Hostess Note: Make half this recipe to serve 12; for 100 use 3 one-pound loaves of bread and 1 pound of butter or margarine.

Cherry Blossoms
These dainty pinwheels, flavored with almonds and cherries, start with unsliced bread. Be sure to order it ahead.
Makes 5 to 6 dozen small sandwiches

1 package (8 ounces) cream cheese
2 tablespoons very finely chopped maraschino cherries
2 tablespoons maraschino-cherry syrup
2 tablespoons very finely chopped toasted slivered almonds (from a 5-ounce can)
1 cup (2 sticks) butter or margarine
1 loaf unsliced fresh white bread

1 Soften cream cheese in a medium-size bowl; blend in cherries, syrup and almonds. Soften butter or margarine until easy to spread in a small bowl.

2 Trim crusts from loaf of bread, then slice bread lengthwise into 8 thin slices. Cover with damp towel; let stand 10 minutes.

3 Spread slices, 1 at a time, with about 2 tablespoons softened butter or margarine, then about 2 tablespoons cheese mixture. Starting at end, roll up, jelly-roll style. Wrap tightly in wax paper, foil or transparent wrap. Chill at least 2 hours, or overnight.

4 To serve, unwrap and slice each roll crosswise into 8 or 9 slices.

Hostess Note: Use your sharpest knife, as bread must be sliced thin and even. We found it easier to cut crusts from bottom, sides and ends, leaving top to hold onto. As you slice rolls, wipe knife often so filling will not smear. For serving 100, make 2 to 3 times the recipe, depending on the varieties of other sandwiches in your tea menu.

Cucumber Towers
Cucumber slices make the crisp filling for these triple-deck sandwiches.
Makes 4 dozen small sandwiches

 1 large cucumber
18 thin slices white bread (about 1 loaf)
 6 tablespoons (¾ stick) butter or margarine, softened
 1 jar (about 4 ounces) tiny pickled onions, drained
 1 can (4 ounces) pimientos, drained and cut into tiny squares or circles

1 Score rind of cucumber with a fork, then cut cucumber into 24 thin slices.

2 Cut 2 rounds from each slice of bread with a 2-inch cutter; spread rounds with butter or margarine, using about a half teaspoonful for each.

3 Make 12 sandwiches, each with 2 slices of cucumber between 3 rounds of bread. Place on tray lined with a damp towel; cover; chill.

4 Thread 2 pickled onions and 2 pieces of pimiento onto sharp end of a wooden pick for

1709

each kebab; place on a plate; cover with wax paper, foil or transparent wrap; chill.

5 When ready to serve, place 4 kebabs in each sandwich round, sticking pick to bottom to hold round together. Cut rounds into quarters with sharp knife.

Hostess Note: These sandwiches are perfect make-aheads if tray is covered and kept chilled. For serving 100, make 3 times the recipe.

Mint Jewels
Ladyfingers are the starter for these little sweet tea sandwiches.
Makes 4 dozen small sandwiches

    8 ladyfingers
    3 tablespoons butter or margarine, softened
    10 preserved kumquats, drained and sliced thin
    1 tablespoon mint jelly

1 Separate ladyfingers to make 16 pieces; spread with softened butter or margarine. Cut each piece crosswise into thirds.
2 Top each with a kumquat slice, then a dot of mint jelly; place in single layer on large plate. Cover wiith wax paper, foil or transparent wrap; chill.

Hostess Note: These little treats are real tempters. They are good keepers, too, even as long as overnight, if covered and chilled. For serving 100, make 3 or 4 times the recipe.

Strawberry Cornucopias
Makes 32 small sandwiches

    3 cups (1½ pints) strawberries
    1 package (8 ounces) cream cheese
    2 tablespoons 10X (confectioners' powdered) sugar
    ¼ cup finely chopped walnuts
    32 slices soft white bread (about two 1-pound loaves)

1 Wash strawberries and hull; mash enough to measure 2 tablespoonfuls in a medium-size bowl; set remainder aside.
2 Beat cream cheese and 10X sugar into mashed strawberries until smooth; stir in walnuts.
3 Cut a round from center of each slice of bread with a 3-inch cookie cutter; roll each thin with a rolling pin. Spread a rounded teaspoonful cream-cheese mixture over each; roll into a cornucopia shape.

1710

4 Halve remaining strawberries; tuck one half into end of each sandwich.

Hostess Note: Sandwiches may be made up about an hour ahead. Place in a single layer on a cookie sheet or tray, cover tightly to prevent drying and chill. Add strawberry garnish just before serving so color doesn't run.

Orange Cream Crescents
Makes 32 small sandwiches

    1 cup apple jelly (from a 10-ounce jar)
    1 can (11 ounces) mandarin-orange segments, drained
    1 package (8 ounces) cream cheese
    1 tablespoon grated orange peel
    1 tablespoon milk
    2 cans (8 ounces each) orange-nut bread

1 Heat jelly just until melted in a small saucepan; remove from heat. Place orange segments, a few at a time, in jelly, turning to coat well; lift out with a fork and place on a wire rack set over wax paper; let stand until jelly sets.
2 Blend cream cheese with orange peel and milk in a small bowl.
3 Slice bread into 16 rounds; halve each. Spread with cheese mixture; top each with 1 large or 2 small mandarin-orange segments.

Hostess Note: Slice bread ahead and wrap tightly. Glaze orange segments and mix cream-cheese topping; cover both and chill, ready to finish sandwiches about an hour before serving.

Jelly Roll-Ups
Makes 2 dozen small sandwiches

    12 thin slices soft white bread
    6 tablespoons softened butter or margarine
    ½ cup currant or raspberry jelly

1 Spread bread smoothly with butter or margarine, then with jelly; cut off crusts; roll up.
2 Place, cut side down and close together, in shallow pan lined with wax paper; cover with foil, or with wax paper and a damp clean towel; chill.
3 To serve, cut each roll in half; arrange on tray.

Hostess Note: Count on about 18 slices to a 1-pound loaf of thin-sliced bread. Be sure it is fresh and soft so rolls won't crack. For 12, make half this recipe; for serving 100, buy 3 loaves and 1 pound of butter or margarine.

Ham Pinwheels and Asparagus Rolls cluster around a vegetable bouquet. Next plate: Cherry-Nut Fingers.

Date-Nut Triangles

With a simple cutting trick, canned date bread filled with fluffy orange "cream" takes on a fancy shape.
Makes 40 small sandwiches

1 package (3 or 4 ounces) cream cheese
1 teaspoon grated orange peel
2 teaspoons orange juice
1 can (8 ounces) date-nut roll

1 Blend cream cheese and orange peel and juice until soft enough to spread in a small bowl.
2 Halve date-nut roll lengthwise; spread one side with half of the cheese mixture; put back together to form a roll. Halve again at right angles to first cut; spread with remaining cheese mixture; put back together. (Roll will be divided into 4 sections separated by the cheese mixture.)
3 Wrap tightly in wax paper, foil or transparent wrap. Chill at least 2 hours, or overnight.
4 When ready to serve, slice roll crosswise into 10 rounds. Lay each flat and cut into quarters, cutting through bread—not filling. Arrange on serving tray.

Cherry-Nut Fingers

For neat slicing, bake the bread the day before, wrap and store.
Bake at 350° for 1 hour. Makes about 4½ dozen sandwiches

2¼ cups sifted all-purpose flour
¾ cup sugar
2 teaspoons baking powder
¾ teaspoon salt
½ teaspoon baking soda
¾ cup chopped maraschino cherries, well drained
½ cup chopped walnuts
1 egg
1 tablespoon grated orange peel
½ cup orange juice
½ cup milk
3 tablespoons melted vegetable shortening
1 container (8 ounces) whipped cream cheese

1 Sift flour, sugar, baking powder, salt and soda into a large bowl; stir in cherries and walnuts.
2 Beat egg in a small bowl; stir in orange peel and juice and milk; add all at once to flour mixture; add melted shortening. Stir just until evenly moistened. Spoon into a well-greased loaf pan, 9x5x3.
3 Bake in moderate oven (350°) 1 hour, or until a wooden pick inserted in center comes out clean. Cool in pan on a wire rack 10 minutes; loosen around edges with a knife; turn out onto rack; cool completely. Wrap loaf in wax paper, foil, or transparent wrap and store overnight for easy slicing.
4 When ready to make sandwiches, trim a thin slice from each end of loaf and set aside for family nibbles. Slice remaining bread ¼ inch thick with a sharp knife. Spread half of the slices with whipped cream cheese, using 1 tablespoon for each; put together with remaining plain slices to make sandwiches. Cut each sandwich crosswise into 4 even strips. Wrap and chill until serving time.

1711

SAUCERY:
BASIC SAUCES, GRAVIES AND GLAZES
FOR BEEF, PORK, VEAL, POULTRY, LAMB,
SEAFOOD AND VEGETABLES

The foundation of many a classic French recipe is a sauce. And the reputation of many a French chef rests upon his skill with saucepan and whisk.

Originally, sauces were invented to disguise dishes (or rather their slightly tainted taste) instead of to embellish them. Today, however, we rely upon sauces to enhance the flavor of a dish. What, for example, would a juicily tender roast be without a gravy prepared from the pan drippings? Or a Newburg without its delicate wine sauce? Or young shoots of asparagus without a ladling of Brown Butter or sunny hollandaise? Or steak minus Béarnaise?

The sauces known today number high in the hundreds. That French culinary classic, *Larousse Gastronomique*, devotes 30 large pages of miniscule type to the subject of sauces and butters. Whole volumes, in fact, have been written about sauces.

What we include here are the basic sauces, the very best that FAMILY CIRCLE has printed over the years. There are sauces for beef, veal, lamb, pork and ham, for poultry and seafood, for vegetables (dessert sauces are included with desserts in VOLUME 7).

Of the sauces that follow, some are quick to make and some, frankly, not so quick. But all are guaranteed to make a good dish better and a better one "the best."

SOME BASIC ALL-PURPOSE SAUCES

Basic Gravy
Does gravy-making baffle you? It needn't; there's really no trick to it. The key to perfect, sparkling-rich gravy is simply accurate measuring. Know how much fat there is in the pan, then blend in the same amount of flour. The rest is easy.
Makes 1 cup

2 tablespoons fat
2 tablespoons all-purpose flour
1 cup water or milk

1 Tip roasting pan enough to let drippings flow into one corner. As fat rises to top, pour off into a bowl, but leave brown bits in pan. Follow measurements above for fat, flour and water needed.
2 Measure fat into pan, then blend in flour, stirring and cooking just until mixture bubbles. Stir in measured water or milk, keeping pan over low heat so mixture doesn't spatter or scorch.
3 Continue cooking, scraping baked-on juices from bottom and sides of pan as you stir, until gravy thickens and boils 1 minute. Season to taste; darken with a bit of bottled gravy coloring; if you wish.

1713

Basic White Sauce
Put away your double boiler and bring out a heavy saucepan, as the secrets of smooth,

One of the loveliest and most versatile of sauces— golden, velvety Hollandaise. It's perfect with asparagus, artichokes, broccoli and snowy cauliflower.

creamy white sauce are just three: Measure accurately, cook slowly and stir constantly. Makes 2 cups White Sauce

Thin Sauce

2 tablespoons fat
2 tablespoons all-purpose flour
½ teaspoon salt
⅛ teaspoon pepper
2 cups milk

Uses: Cream soups, chowders, casseroles, sauces

Medium Sauce

4 tablespoons fat
4 tablespoons all-purpose flour
½ teaspoon salt
⅛ teaspoon pepper
2 cups milk

Uses: Creamed dishes, sauces, gravies

Thick Sauce

6 tablespoons fat
6 tablespoons all-purpose flour
½ teaspoon salt
⅛ teaspoon pepper
2 cups milk

Uses: Soufflés, croquettes, patties

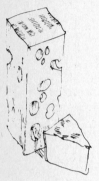

1 Melt butter or margarine over *low* heat in small saucepan. Watch it, as it should just melt—not bubble and turn brown. (We like a wooden spoon for stirring).
2 Have flour, salt and pepper measured and ready. Stir quickly into melted butter, then cook, stirring all the time, just until it bubbles and is rich and buttery.
3 Now stir in milk *slowly.* (This helps to keep sauce from lumping.) Continue cooking and stirring from bottom of pan until sauce thickens and boils 1 minute.

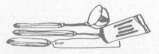

SOME SAUCES DESCENDED FROM BASIC WHITE SAUCE

New Delhi Cream—Blend ½ cup mayonnaise, ½ teaspoon grated onion and ¼ teaspoon curry powder into 1 cup hot THIN WHITE SAUCE. Delicious on green peas.
Makes 1½ cups.

Spring Egg Sauce—Stir 1 chopped hard-cooked egg, 1 tablespoon cut chives and a dash of seasoned salt into 1 cup hot THIN WHITE SAUCE. Serve over cooked, well-drained spinach. Makes 1¼ cups.

Pink Sauce—Stir 2 tablespoons catsup and 2 teaspoons prepared horseradish into 1 cup

hot THIN WHITE SAUCE. Spoon over a freshly cooked head of cauliflower. Makes about 1 cup.

Old-Fashioned Cheese Sauce—Stir 1 cup (¼ pound) grated mild or sharp Cheddar cheese and ¼ teaspoon dry mustard into 1 cup hot THIN WHITE SAUCE. Serve over cauliflower, broccoli or green beans. Also good over poached fish fillets. Makes 1¼ cups.

Exotic Herb Sauce—Stir 1 teaspoon onion-herb salad-dressing mix into 1 cup hot THIN WHITE SAUCE. Serve over boiled carrots. Makes 1 cup.

Anchovy Sauce—Blend 1 teaspoon anchovy paste into 1 cup hot THIN WHITE SAUCE. Serve over freshly boiled potatoes or green peas. Makes 1 cup.

TWO BASIC CHEESE SAUCES

Cheese Sauce
Versatile American is the starter for this trio of toppers.
Makes about 1½ cups

2 tablespoons butter or margarine
2 tablespoons all-purpose flour
½ teaspoon dry mustard
¼ teaspoon salt
⅛ teaspoon seasoned pepper
1 cup milk
1 teaspoon Worcestershire sauce
1 cup shredded process American cheese

1 Melt butter or margarine in a small saucepan; stir in flour, mustard, salt and seasoned pepper; cook, stirring constantly, until bubbly.
2 Stir in milk and Worcestershire sauce; continue cooking and stirring until sauce thickens and boils 1 minute. Stir in cheese until melted. Serve hot over broccoli, green beans or cauliflower.

CHILI-CHEESE SAUCE—Prepare recipe above, using ½ cup beef broth and 1 can (about 8 ounces) chili-without-beans instead of milk. Serve hot over frankfurters or hamburgers. Makes about 2 cups.

TOMATO-CHEESE SAUCE—Prepare recipe above, using only ½ cup milk; stir in 1 can (6 ounces) tomato juice. Serve hot over sliced hard-cooked eggs on toast. Makes about 1¾ cups.

Mornay Sauce
Swiss cheese seasons this classic; Parmesan goes into its variation.
Makes about 1⅓ cups

1 tablespoon butter or margarine
1 tablespoon all-purpose flour
⅛ teaspoon white pepper
1 small can evaporated milk (⅔ cup)
⅔ cup water
1 envelope instant chicken broth
    OR: 1 teaspoon granulated chicken bouillon
1 egg yolk
½ cup shredded Swiss cheese

1 Melt butter or margarine in a small saucepan; stir in flour and pepper. Cook, stirring constantly, until bubbly. Stir in evaporated milk, water and chicken broth; continue cooking and stirring until mixture thickens and boils 1 minute.

2 Beat egg yolk slightly in a small bowl; slowly beat in half of the hot mixture, then beat back into remaining mixture in pan. Cook, stirring constantly, 1 minute. (Do not boil.) Stir in cheese until melted. Serve hot over poached fish.

PARMESAN SAUCE—Prepare recipe above, using only ⅓ cup water and ¼ cup grated Parmesan cheese instead of Swiss. Stir in ¼ cup chopped parsley. Serve hot over baked potatoes. Makes about 1 cup.

SOME BASIC BUTTER SAUCES

Savory Butter Sauces:

Herb Butter—Melt 1 stick (¼ pound) butter or margarine over moderate heat; stir in 1 tablespoon chopped fresh chives, chervil, marjoram, parsley or tarragon. Good over broiled fish or boiled vegetables. Makes ½ cup.

Paprika Butter—Melt 1 stick (¼ pound) butter or margarine over moderate heat; mix in 2 to 3 teaspoons paprika. Good over broiled fish, boiled potatoes or corn-on-the-cob. Makes ½ cup.

Curry Butter—Placé 1 stick (¼ pound) butter or margarine and 1 tablespoon curry powder in a small saucepan; heat over moderate heat just until melted. Good over broiled fish, stewed broccoli, cauliflower or asparagus. Makes ½ cup.

Chili Butter—Place 1 stick (¼ pound) butter or margarine and 1 tablespoon chili powder in a small saucepan; heat over moderate heat just until melted. Good over broiled fish, boiled corn-on-the-cob. Makes ½ cup.

Mustard Butter—Melt 1 stick (¼ pound) butter or margarine over moderate heat; mix in 2 teaspoons lemon juice, ½ teaspoon salt and ¼ teaspoon dry mustard. Good over steamed asparagus or broccoli. Makes ½ cup.

Garlic Butter—Place 1 stick (¼ pound) butter or margarine and ½ to 1 clove minced garlic (depending on how well you like garlic) in a small saucepan; heat over moderate heat until melted. Strain butter. Good with boiled lobster, also as a spread for bread. Makes ½ cup.

Shallot Butter—Place 1 stick (¼ pound) butter or margarine and 1 to 2 minced shallots in a small saucepan; heat over moderate heat until melted. Good with broiled fish, boiled green beans and peas. Makes ½ cup.

Parmesan Butter—Melt 1 stick (¼ pound) butter or margarine over moderate heat; sprinkle in 1 tablespoon freshly grated Parmesan cheese. Delicious with cooked broccoli, cauliflower and asparagus. Also with green beans. Makes ½ cup.

Almond Butter—Melt 1 stick (¼ pound) butter or margarine over moderate heat; stir in ½ cup toasted slivered almonds. Serve over broiled fish, tossed with cooked green beans or drizzled over steamed broccoli, cauliflower or asparagus. Makes about ¾ cup.

Pecan Butter—Melt 1 stick (¼ pound) butter or margarine over moderate heat; stir in 2 tablespoons chopped pecans. Good with steamed broccoli, cauliflower, asparagus or green beans. Makes ½ cup.

Brown Butter Sauces:

Brown Butter (Beurre Noir)—Melt 1 stick (¼ pound) butter or margarine over moderate heat, then continue heating until it bubbles and turns the color of topaz. Serve over broiled fish, steamed asparagus or cauliflower. Makes ½ cup.

Worcestershire Butter—Prepare BROWN BUTTER as directed and just before serving, stir in 1 to 2 teaspoons Worcestershire sauce. Delicious over steamed cauliflower. Makes ½ cup.

Brown Butter Piquant—Prepare BROWN BUTTER as directed and just before serving, stir in 2 teaspoons cut chives, 1 teaspoon lemon juice, ¼ teaspoon ground nutmeg, ¼ teaspoon salt and ⅛ teaspoon freshly ground pepper. Serve over steamed cauliflower, broccoli or asparagus. Makes ½ cup.

Brown Butter Amandine—Place 1 stick (¼

1715

pound) butter or margarine and 2 tablespoons blanched slivered almonds in a small skillet and heat, slowly, shaking pan often, just until butter or margarine bubbles and turns golden-brown; remove from heat. Stir in 1 tablespoon lemon juice and ¼ teaspoon salt. Serve over broiled fish fillets, steamed broccoli, asparagus or cauliflower. Makes ½ cup.

Brown Butter Sesame—Place 1 stick (¼ pound) butter or margarine and 2 tablespoons sesame seeds in a small skillet and heat slowly, shaking pan often, just until butter or margarine bubbles and turns golden-brown; mix in 1 tablespoon sugar, 1 tablespoon soy sauce and 1 tablespoon cider vinegar. Serve over cooked green beans, spinach, broccoli or carrots. Makes about ⅔ cup.

SOME BASIC SOUR CREAM SAUCES

Keep a carton of dairy sour cream in the refrigerator and you will have a variety of instant sauces at hand. Here are some of the best:

Chive–Sour Cream Sauce—Mix 1 tablespoon snipped chives into 1 cup dairy sour cream. Delicious on baked potatoes. Makes 1 cup.

Caraway Cream—Stir 1 teaspoon caraway seeds into 1 cup dairy sour cream along with 1 teaspoon Worcestershire sauce and ¼ salt. Delicious with cooked shredded green or red cabbage. Makes 1 cup.

Cucumber Cream—Blend 2 tablespoons each mayonnaise and lemon juice, 1 tablespoon sugar, ½ teaspoon onion salt and a few drops liquid red pepper seasoning into 1 cup dairy sour cream. Finely chop the white part of 1 pared medium-size cucumber (no seeds) and stir in. Serve on mild-flavor zucchini or yellow squash. Makes about 1½ cups.

Horseradish Cream—Stir 1 tablespoon each prepared horseradish and chili sauce and 1 teaspoon prepared mustard into 1 cup dairy sour cream. Superb with boiled beef or tongue, with ham, with boiled onions. Makes about 1 cup.

Zippy Hot Mustard Cream—Blend 2 tablespoons spicy brown prepared mustard and 1 tablespoon prepared horseradish into 1 cup dairy sour cream. Serve with ham or tongue. Makes about 1 cup.

Curry Cream—Stir ½ cup finely chopped celery, 1 teaspoon minced onion and ¼ teaspoon curry powder into 1 cup dairy sour cream. Season to taste with salt and pepper. Spoon over cooked hot green beans, asparagus or broccoli. Makes about 1¼ cups.

1716

SOME BASIC MAYONNAISE SAUCES

Creamy Caper Sauce—Stir ¼ cup light or table cream and 1 tablespoon drained chopped capers into ¼ cup mayonnaise in a small bowl. Spoon over freshly cooked potatoes. Makes about ½ cup.

Deviled Egg Sauce—Combine ½ cup mayonnaise, 3 tablespoons milk and 1 teaspoon prepared mustard in a small saucepan. Heat, stirring constantly, just until bubbly, then stir in 1 chopped hard-cooked egg. Serve over any green vegetable. Makes about ½ cup.

Caesar Sauce—Toast ¾ cup tiny bread cubes in 1 tablespoon butter or margarine in a small frying pan. Stir in 1 tablespoon bottled Caesar salad dressing, then fold in ½ cup mayonnaise. This is a spreadable sauce—delicious on asparagus or cauliflower. Makes about ¾ cup.

Blue-Cheese Sauce—Blend 2 tablespoons blue cheese and ½ teaspoon dry mustard into ½ cup mayonnaise. Serve over asparagus, broccoli, green beans or cauliflower. Makes about ½ cup.

Puffed Derby Sauce—Beat 1 egg white until stiff in a small bowl; fold in ½ cup mayonnaise, 1 tablespoon lemon juice and a dash of nutmeg. Layer over hot vegetable (asparagus, broccoli, lima beans, green beans or squash) in a heat-proof serving dish. Slide into heated broiler for 2 to 3 minutes, or until top is puffed and golden-brown. Makes about 1 cup.

SOME GLAZES FOR MEATS AND POULTRY

Orange-Honey Glaze—Mix 1 can (6 ounces) thawed frozen concentrated orange juice with ¾ cup honey and 1 teaspoon Worcestershire sauce. Use to baste a whole ham or large turkey, applying about every 10 minutes during the last hour of cooking. Makes about 1½ cups.

Old-Time Brown Sugar Glaze—Combine 1 cup firmly packed light brown sugar, 1 teaspoon dry mustard, ¼ teaspoon ground cloves and 2 tablespoons vinegar in a bowl. Use to glaze a whole pre-cooked ham or tongue, patting on before baking. Makes about 1¼ cups.

Pineapple-Curry Glaze—Mix 1 cup pineapple preserves, ¼ cup dill-pickle juice (from jar of pickles) and 1 teaspoon curry powder. Spread on a whole smoked or fresh ham during last hour of cooking. Makes about 1¼ cups.

Currant Jelly Glaze—Soften 1 cup currant jelly

with 2 tablespoons hot water; stir in 2 tablespoons prepared mustard and ¼ teaspoon ground cloves. Brush over a smoked or fresh ham or turkey during final hour of cooking. Also good over leg of lamb or a large veal roast. Makes 1¼ cups.

Ginger-Marmalade Glaze—Blend together ¼ cup orange marmalade, 1 teaspoon sweet-pickle juice (from jar of pickles) and ⅛ teaspoon each ground ginger and allspice. Brush over ham steak before baking. Makes about ¼ cup.

SOME SAUCES FOR BEEF

Béarnaise Sauce
A classic for beef, it tastes equally delicious on lamb or veal.
Makes about 1 cup.

- 1 tablespoon minced onion
- ½ teaspoon leaf tarragon, crumbled
- ⅛ teaspoon pepper
- ½ cup dry white wine
- 1 tablespoon tarragon vinegar
- 2 egg yolks
- ½ cup (1 stick) butter or margarine, melted
   Dash of cayenne
- 1 teaspoon chopped parsley

1 Combine onion, tarragon, pepper, wine and vinegar in a small saucepan. Heat to boiling, then simmer, uncovered, 8 to 10 minutes, or until liquid measures about ⅓ cup. Strain into a cup.

2 Beat egg yolks slightly in the top of a double boiler; stir in about ⅓ of the melted butter or margarine. Place over *simmering* water.

3 Beat in strained liquid, alternately with remaining butter or margarine; continue beating until mixture is fluffy-thick. Remove from heat at once. Stir in cayenne and parsley.

Mock Béarnaise Sauce
A classic sauce for steak, filet-mignon style.
Makes about 1 cup

- ½ cup apple juice
- 1 tablespoon tarragon vinegar
- 1 tablespoon finely chopped onion or shallots
- ⅛ teaspoon freshly ground pepper
- 1 sprig of parsley
- ½ teaspoon leaf tarragon, crumbled
- 2 egg yolks

Béarnaise Sauce is exquisite with almost any steak.

- ½ cup (1 stick) butter or margarine, melted
   Dash of cayenne
- 1 teaspoon chopped parsley

1 Combine apple juice, vinegar, onion or shallots, pepper, parsley sprig and tarragon in a small saucepan. Heat to boiling, then simmer, uncovered, 8 to 10 minutes, or until liquid measures about ⅓ cup; strain into a cup to use in Step 3.

2 Beat egg yolks slightly in top of a double boiler; stir in about ⅓ of the melted butter or margarine. Place top over simmering, *not boiling*, water.
3 Beat in strained liquid, alternately with remaining melted butter or margarine; continue beating, keeping top over simmering water, until mixture is thick and fluffy. Remove from heat at once.
4 Stir in cayenne and chopped parsley. Serve warm.

●

Quick Bordelaise Sauce
Canned mushroom gravy speeds the making of this popular sauce for London broil, hamburger or roast beef.
Makes 2 cups

  1 can (about 10 ounces) mushroom gravy
  1 can (6 ounces) sliced mushrooms
  1 tablespoon grated onion
  2 tablespoons butter or margarine
  1 teaspoon cider vinegar
  ¼ teaspoon leaf thyme, crumbled
  1 bay leaf
  ¼ cup chopped parsley

1 Combine mushroom gravy, mushrooms and liquid, onion, butter or margarine, vinegar, thyme and bay leaf in a small saucepan. Heat to boiling, then simmer 15 minutes to season and blend flavors.
2 Remove bay leaf; stir in parsley. Serve hot.

●

Mushroom-Diable Sauce
Serve this rich savory brown sauce over popular broiled steak.
Makes about 1⅓ cups
  2 tablespoons minced onion
  ¼ cup dry red wine
  1 can (about 11 ounces) mushroom gravy
  ½ teaspoon coarsely ground pepper
  1 teaspoon Worcestershire sauce
  2 tablespoons chopped parsley

1 Combine onion and wine in a small saucepan. Heat to boiling, then simmer 3 minutes, or until onion is soft.
2 Stir in gravy, pepper and Worcestershire sauce. Heat, stirring often, just to boiling.
3 Just before serving, stir in parsley.

●

Horseradish-Almond Sauce
So good with beef pot roast, boiled beef or tongue.
Makes about 1¼ cups

  ¼ cup toasted slivered almonds (from a 5-ounce can)
  2 teaspoons butter or margarine
  2 teaspoons all-purpose flour
  1 teaspoon sugar
  ¼ teaspoon salt
  1 small can evaporated milk (⅔ cup)
  ⅓ cup milk
  2 tablespoons prepared horseradish

1 Sauté almonds in butter or margarine until golden-brown in a small saucepan; remove from heat.
2 Stir in flour, sugar and salt; cook, stirring all the time, just until mixture bubbles. Stir in evaporated milk and milk slowly; continue cooking and stirring until sauce thickens and boils 1 minute.
3 Stir in horseradish; serve warm.

SOME SAUCES FOR PORK, HAM AND TONGUE

Mandarin-Raisin Sauce
Good with baked ham, tongue, fresh or smoked pork-shoulder pot roast.
Makes 3 cups

  ½ cup firmly packed brown sugar
  2 tablespoons cornstarch
  2 envelopes instant chicken broth
  2 cups water
  ½ cup golden raisins
  2 teaspoons grated lemon peel
  ¼ cup lemon juice
  ¼ cup toasted slivered almonds (from a 5-ounce can)
  ¼ cup mandarin-orange segments, drained (from an about-11-ounce can)

1 Mix brown sugar, cornstarch and instant chicken broth in a 1-cup measure.
2 Heat water, raisins, lemon peel and juice to boiling in a medium-size saucepan; remove from heat.
3 Stir in sugar mixture slowly; cook, stirring all the time, until mixture thickens and boils 3 minutes.
4 Stir in almonds and orange segments. Serve hot.

●

Mandarin Meat Sauce
Makes about 3 cups

  1 can (11 ounces) mandarin-orange segments
  2 tablespoons cornstarch

Mandarin-Raisin Sauce is a sweet-sour topping that puts a golden, crowning touch on ham, tongue or pork.

1 can (6 ounces) frozen concentrate for orange juice, thawed
1 clove garlic, halved
⅛ teaspoon ground allspice
2 tablespoons butter or margarine
1 tablespoon lemon juice

1 Drain liquid from mandarin-orange segments into a 2-cup measure; add water to make 1¼ cups. Stir into cornstarch in a medium-size saucepan; stir in orange concentrate, garlic and allspice.
2 Cook, stirring constantly, until mixture thickens and boils 3 minutes; remove garlic and discard. Stir in butter or margarine until melted, lemon juice and orange segments; heat just until hot.
3 Serve hot over baked ham or sliced tongue.

Mustard Sauce
For a treat, dress ham, pork or tongue with this spicy sweet-sour topper.
Makes about 1⅔ cups

3 tablespoons butter or margarine
3 tablespoons all-purpose flour
½ teaspoon salt
1 can (10½ ounces) condensed beef broth
¼ cup prepared horseradish mustard
2 tablespoons light brown sugar

1 Melt butter or margarine in a small saucepan; stir in flour and salt. Cook, stirring constantly, until bubbly.
2 Stir in beef broth; continue cooking and stirring until sauce thickens and boils 1 minute. Stir in mustard and brown sugar. (Store any leftover sauce in a covered jar in the refrigerator to reheat for another meal.)

Javanese Peanut Sauce
Peanut butter is the base of this mild sauce. Serve with baked spareribs or pork chops.
Makes 1¼ cups

1 small onion, chopped (¼ cup)
2 tablespoons peanut oil or vegetable oil
¼ teaspoon ground cardamom
½ cup cream-style peanut butter
¼ cup firmly packed brown sugar
¼ cup soy sauce
¼ cup lemon juice
¼ teaspoon liquid red pepper seasoning

1 Sauté onion in peanut oil or vegetable oil just until soft in a small frying pan; stir in cardamom. Let stand to cool slightly.
2 Blend peanut butter with brown sugar in a small bowl; stir in remaining ingredients, then cooled onion mixture.
3 Let stand at room temperature until serving time.

Cumberland Sauce
Slightly sweet, slightly spicy and so good with roast loin of pork, ham or tongue.
Makes 1 cup

⅔ cup currant jelly
1 tablespoon grated lemon peel
¼ cup lemon juice
1 teaspoon grated onion
1 teaspoon dry mustard
½ teaspoon ground ginger

Combine all ingredients in a small saucepan; heat slowly, stirring constantly, just until jelly melts and sauce is blended. Serve warm.

SOME SAUCES FOR VEAL

Italian Tomato Sauce
Use this versatile sauce with veal balls and spaghetti or in any dish that takes Italian-style tomato sauce.
Makes about 3½ cups

1 medium-size onion, chopped (½ cup)
1 clove of garlic, minced
2 tablespoons olive oil or vegetable oil
1 can (about 1 pound) Italian tomatoes
1 can (8 ounces) tomato sauce
1 envelope spaghetti-sauce mix without tomatoes
1 teaspoon sugar

1 Sauté onion and garlic in olive oil or vegetable oil just until soft in a medium-size saucepan.
2 Stir in remaining ingredients. Simmer, stirring several times, 30 minutes, or until slightly thick.

Olive Sauce-Gravy
When you fix your favorite veal roast, make this piquant topper to serve with it.
Makes 2 cups

Roast veal drippings
3 tablespoons all-purpose flour
2 cups water
1 tablespoon bottled savory sauce
¼ cup sliced stuffed olives

1 Prepare and cook your favorite veal roast; remove meat and rack from pan.
2 Tip pan and let fat rise in one corner; pour off all fat into a cup, leaving drippings in pan.
3 Return 3 tablespoons fat to pan; blend in flour; cook, stirring all the time, just until mixture bubbles.
4 Stir in water slowly; continue cooking and stirring, scraping baked-on juices from bottom and sides of pan, until mixture thickens and boils 1 minute.
5 Stir in savory sauce and olives. Season with salt and pepper, if needed.

Stroganoff Sauce
It's delicious with sautéed veal cutlets or chops. Or, cube leftover roast veal, heat in sauce and serve over noodles.
Makes 3 cups

1 small onion, chopped (¼ cup)
1 tablespoon butter or margarine
1 can (about 11 ounces) chicken gravy
1 can (3 or 4 ounces) sliced mushrooms, drained
1 cup dairy sour cream

1 Sauté onion in butter or margarine just until soft in a small saucepan; stir in chicken gravy and mushrooms. Heat, stirring constantly, just to boiling; remove from heat.
2 Just before serving, blend in sour cream *very slowly.* Heat, stirring constantly, *just until hot.*

SOME SAUCES FOR LAMB

Curry Sauce
Use this basic sauce to turn leftover lamb, veal or chicken into a favorite curry dish. Recipe makes lots, but it halves easily.
Makes 6 cups

2 large onions, chopped (2 cups)
2 cloves of garlic, minced

3 tablespoons vegetable oil
2 tablespoons curry powder
2 teaspoons ground allspice
2 teaspoons salt
1 teaspoon ground coriander
2 jars (about 8 ounces each) junior prunes
2 jars (about 8 ounces each) junior apples-and-apricots
1½ cups water
¼ cup lemon juice
½ cup chopped bottled chutney

1 Sauté onions and garlic in vegetable oil until soft in a large heavy saucepan; stir in curry powder, allspice, salt and coriander. Continue cooking, stirring constantly, about 2 minutes.
2 Stir in fruits, water and lemon juice. Simmer, uncovered, stirring often, 30 minutes to season and blend flavors; remove from heat, then stir in chutney.
3 Heat your choice of diced cooked meat in sauce to spoon over cooked rice. (1 cup of meat to each 1½ cups of sauce is a good measure to follow.)

Caper Sauce
Gravy-sauce mix is your speedy helper for this mildly seasoned topper for braised lamb shoulder or lamb pot roast.
Makes 1½ cups

1 envelope (about 1 ounce) golden gravy--sauce mix
2 tablespoons drained capers
1 teaspoon grated onion

1 Prepare gravy-sauce mix with milk and water, following label directions for basic gravy-sauce.
2 Stir in capers and onion; cook about 2 minutes longer. Serve hot.

Orange-Mint Sauce
Marmalade, mustard and mint blend invitingly in this different go-with for hot or cold roast lamb or broiled chops.
Makes ¾ cup

1721

Combine ½ cup orange marmalade and ¼ cup prepared mustard in a small saucepan; heat slowly just until marmalade melts. Stir in ¼ cup chopped fresh mint. Serve warm or cold.

Cheese sauce is so versatile. It partners with broccoli, asparagus, green or wax beans, with fish and eggs, even with toast (à la rarebit). Best of all, it can be ladled on, then browned under the broiler.

SOME SAUCES FOR POULTRY

1722

Supreme Sauce
Sauce goes on in two layers, then into the broiler to puff up and brown.
Makes 4 servings

1 tablespoon finely chopped onion
5 tablespoons butter or margarine
5 tablespoons all-purpose flour
½ teaspoon salt
⅛ teaspoon pepper
1 chicken-bouillon cube
2 cups milk
4 tablespoons grated Parmesan cheese
2 tablespoons cream for whipping

1 Sauté onion in butter or margarine just until soft in a small heavy saucepan; stir in flour, salt and pepper; cook, stirring all the time, over low heat just until mixture bubbles; add bouillon cube.
2 Stir in milk slowly; continue cooking and stirring until bouillon cube dissolves and sauce thickens and boils 1 minute. Stir in 2 tablespoons of the cheese. (Set remaining cheese aside for Step 4.)
3 Measure out ½ cup sauce and set aside for next step; spoon remaining over cooked vegetable and chicken or turkey slices on a broiler-proof platter.
4 Beat cream until stiff in a small bowl; fold into saved ½ cup sauce; spoon over first layer of sauce. Sprinkle with saved 2 tablespoons of Parmesan cheese.

5 Broil, about 4 inches from heat, 3 to 5 minutes, or until sauce puffs and browns. Serve at once.

●

Barbecue Sauce

Simply spoon over chicken and bake. Perfect too, on oven-cooked spareribs.
Makes 2½ cups

2 cans (8 ounces each) tomato sauce
1 medium-size onion, chopped (½ cup)
1 clove of garlic, minced
¼ cup soy sauce
2 tablespoons sugar
1 teaspoon dry mustard
⅛ teaspoon cayenne

1 Mix all ingredients in a medium-size bowl.
2 Spoon over chicken halves or pieces, then bake. (Store any leftover sauce in a covered jar in the refrigerator.

●

Plum Sauce

It's sweet, yet spicily sharp—a perfect combination for rich-flavored duck.
Makes 1 cup

1 cup plum jam
1 tablespoon cider vinegar
1 teaspoon grated onion
½ teaspoon ground allspice
¼ teaspoon ground ginger
  Dash of cayenne

1 Combine all ingredients in small saucepan; heat, stirring constantly, just to boiling.
2 Cool, then chill. This sauce keeps well in the refrigerator.

●

Dark Cherry Sauce

Perfect with roast duck or crisply broiled chicken. Or serve it with roast pork.
Makes about 2 cups

1 can (1 pound) pitted dark sweet cherries
2 tablespoons cornstarch
1 tablespoon prepared mustard
1 tablespoon molasses
  Few drops liquid red pepper seasoning
  Dash of salt
3 tablespoons lemon juice

1 Drain syrup from cherries into a 2-cup measure; add water to make 1½ cups. (Save cherries for Step 3.)
2 Blend a few tablespoons syrup into cornstarch until smooth in a small saucepan; stir

in remaining syrup, mustard, molasses, liquid red pepper seasoning and salt. Cook over low heat, stirring constantly, until mixture thickens and boils 3 minutes.
3 Stir in cherries and lemon juice; heat slowly just until bubbly. Serve hot.

●

Cape Cod Sauce

Any left over? Store it in a covered jar in the refrigerator for your next cookout.
Makes 2⅓ cups

1 can (1 pound) jellied cranberry sauce
½ cup sugar
1 tablespoon curry powder
1 teaspoon salt
1 teaspoon ground cardamom
½ teaspoon ground ginger
½ cup cider vinegar
2 tablespoons molasses
1 tablespoon Worcestershire sauce

1 Break up cranberry sauce with a fork in medium-size saucepan; blend in remaining ingredients.
2 Heat to boiling; simmer 5 minutes, stirring often; remove from heat; beat with rotary beater until blended.

SOME SAUCES FOR SEAFOOD

Newburg Sauce

This favorite with shrimps, lobster or crab goes together quickly with frozen soup.
Makes 3 cups

2 cans (10 ounces each) frozen cream of
  shrimp soup
½ cup light cream or table cream
4 egg yolks
¼ cup dry sherry
  OR: 2 tablespoons lemon juice

1 Thaw shrimp soup with cream in top of a double boiler over simmering water; stir until well blended.
2 Beat egg yolks slightly with a fork in a small bowl. Stir in a generous ½ cup of hot soup mixture, then stir back into remaining in double boiler; stir in sherry or lemon juice. Cook, stirring constantly, 2 minutes; remove top from hot water.

3 Stir in your choice of cooked shrimps, or lobster or crabmeat chunks (2 cups is a good measure); reheat, stirring often, over simmering water, just until hot. Serve at once over toast or cooked rice or noodles as sauce may curdle if it stands over hot water too long.

Tartare Sauce
Perfect on just about any kind of broiled, baked or poached fish.
Makes 1½ cups or enough for 2 pounds of fish

Beat 2 egg whites until they stand in stiff peaks in a medium-size bowl; fold in ½ cup bottled tartare sauce. Spoon in a layer over cooked fish in a broilerproof baking dish. Broil, about 4 inches from heat, 3 to 5 minutes, or until puffed and golden.

Swiss Tartare Sauce
Cheese gives it a mellow flavor. Serve on seafood, cauliflower, broccoli or asparagus.
Makes about 1 cup

½ cup mayonnaise or salad dressing
¼ cup grated Swiss cheese
2 tablespoons sweet-pickle relish
1 tablespoon catsup
¼ teaspoon instant minced onion

Blend all ingredients in a small bowl. Serve at room temperature.

Dill Butter
It doubles as a seasoner to brush on salmon or halibut steaks as they cook and as a sauce to spoon on just before serving.
Makes ½ cup

Melt ½ cup (1 stick) butter or margarine in a small saucepan; stir in 2 tablespoons lemon juice and 1 teaspoon dillweed. Brush over fish while broiling, then spoon any remaining on top before serving.

Creamy Curry Sauce
Makes 1⅓ cups sauce

½ cup mayonnaise or salad dressing
2 tablespoons all-purpose flour
1 teaspoon curry powder

¼ teaspoon salt
1 cup milk

1 Blend mayonnaise or salad dressing, flour, curry powder and salt in small saucepan; gradually stir in milk.
2 Cook over low heat, stirring constantly, 5 minutes, or until sauce thickens slightly; serve hot over broiled, baked or poached fish.

SOME SAUCES FOR VEGETABLES

Fluffy Hollandaise Sauce
Makes about 1⅔ cups

½ cup (1 stick) butter or margarine
¼ cup hot water
4 egg yolks
2 tablespoons lemon juice
¼ teaspoon salt
   Dash of cayenne

1 Melt butter or margarine in top of a double boiler over simmering water; stir in hot water. Remove top from heat and set on work surface.
2 Add unbeaten egg yolks all at once; beat with electric or rotary beater 2 to 3 minutes, or until mixture is almost double in bulk. Stir in lemon juice, salt and cayenne.
3 Place over simmering water again; cook, stirring constantly, 5 minutes, or until thickened. (Be sure water in lower part does not touch bottom of upper part or boil at any time during cooking.)
4 Remove sauce from heat; let stand, uncovered, until serving time. To reheat: Place over simmering water again and stir lightly for 2 to 3 minutes. (In reheating, sauce may lose some of its fluffiness but it will keep its golden-rich creaminess.)

SOME HOLLANDAISE DESCENDANTS

Hollandaise, with its tart buttery flavor, is an ideal topper for almost any vegetable. And it isn't difficult to make. Nor are the three hollandaise-based sauces that follow.

Mousseline Sauce
Light and fluffy and ever-so-good ·on spinach, cauliflower, broccoli and asparagus.

1724

Mousseline Sauce can be considered a daughter of Hollandaise. Whipped cream is the magic ingredient, folded in after a Hollandaise is prepared.

Prepare half of the recipe for FLUFFY HOLLANDAISE SAUCE *(recipe precedes)*. Fold in ¼ cup cream, whipped. Heat over simmering water, stirring lightly once or twice just until hot. Makes 1½ cups.

Figaro Sauce
Delicious as a sauce for broccoli or cauliflower or as a dip for hot artichokes.

Prepare half of the recipe for FLUFFY HOLLANDAISE SAUCE *(recipe precedes)*. Lightly fold in 1 tablespoon bottled barbecue sauce. Makes about 1 cup.

Springtime Sauce
Great over baked or freshly boiled potatoes, also mixed into drained hot green peas.

Prepare half of the recipe for FLUFFY HOLLANDAISE SAUCE *(recipe precedes)*. Lightly fold in ½ cup cream that has been beaten to soft peaks and 2 teaspoons finely cut chives. Makes about 2 cups.

Mock Hollandaise
Splendid trio of sauces starts with mayonnaise or salad dressing.
Makes about 1¼ cups

1725

¾ cup mayonnaise or salad dressing
½ cup milk
1 tablespoon lemon juice
½ teaspoon salt
⅛ teaspoon pepper

Combine all ingredients in a small saucepan. Heat slowly, stirring constantly, just until hot. Serve hot over cooked asparagus.

CURRY À LA CRÈME—Combine ¾ cup mayonnaise or salad dressing, ½ cup milk and 1 teaspoon curry powder in a small saucepan. Heat slowly, stirring constantly, just until hot. Serve hot over cooked whole onions. Makes about 1¼ cups.

SAVORY MUSTARD—Combine ¾ cup mayonnaise or salad dressing, ¼ cup milk and 2 tablespoons prepared horseradish-mustard in a small saucepan. Heat slowly, stirring constantly, just until hot. Serve hot over cooked carrots. Makes about 1 cup.

Gourmet White Sauce
Probably the most familiar and versatile of all sauces, and it takes to almost any seasoning dress-up, any vegetable.
Makes 2 cups

4 tablespoons (½ stick) butter or margarine
4 tablespoons all-purpose flour
½ teaspoon salt
⅛ teaspoon pepper
1 cup milk
1 cup light cream or table cream

1 Melt butter or margarine in a small heavy saucepan over low heat; stir in flour, salt and pepper; cook, stirring all the time, just until mixture bubbles.
2 Stir in milk and cream slowly; continue cooking and stirring until sauce thickens and boils 1 minute.

1726

Goldenrod Sauce
Try this sunny topper on green beans, spinach, broccoli or baked potatoes.
Makes about 1½ cups

Prepare half of the recipe for GOURMET WHITE SAUCE (recipe precedes) to make 1 cup. Or prepare with your favorite white-sauce mix, following label directions. Stir in 1 hard-cooked egg, shelled and chopped fine, and 1 teaspoon prepared mustard.

Caribbean Sauce
A "secret ingredient" adds an elusive flavor. Serve on boiled onions, asparagus, cooked cucumbers, braised celery or cabbage.
Makes 1 cup

Prepare half of the recipe for GOURMET WHITE SAUCE (recipe precedes) to make 1 cup. Or prepare with your favorite white-sauce mix, following label directions, Stir in ¼ teaspoon bottled aromatic bitters.

Dill Cream
Sauces of sour cream take just a bit of seasoning, a little chilling time.
Makes about 1¼ cups

1 cup (8-ounce carton) dairy sour cream
¼ cup chopped pared cucumber
1 tablespoon lemon juice
1 teaspoon dillweed
¼ teaspoon salt
⅛ teaspoon pepper

Combine all ingredients in a small bowl; chill at least 30 minutes. Serve cold over hot boiled potatoes.

ONION CREAM—Combine 1 cup dairy sour cream, ½ teaspoon seasoned salt and ¼ teaspoon seasoned pepper in a small bowl; beat until fluffy. Fold in 2 tablespoons chopped green onion; chill at least 30 minutes. Serve cold over cold cooked beets. Makes about 1⅔ cups.

RELISH CREAM—Combine 1 cup dairy sour cream, ¼ cup sweet-pickle relish and 1 teaspoon celery salt in a small bowl; chill at least 30 minutes. Serve cold over hot cooked lima beans. Makes about 1¼ cups.

Guacamole Sauce
Serve over hearts of lettuce, as a topper for baked potatoes or broccoli or as a dip for raw vegetables.
Makes about 2 cups

1 teaspoon salt
1 medium-size ripe avocado, peeled and pitted
¼ cup mayonnaise or salad dressing
¼ cup lemon juice
1 teaspoon grated onion
⅛ teaspoon liquid red pepper seasoning
1 large tomato, peeled, chopped and drained

1 Mash avocado in a small bowl. (There should be about 1 cup pulp.)
2 Blend in remaining ingredients. Cover tightly; chill. (Sauce will keep its bright green color for several hours before serving.)

Watercress Cream

Tart and peppy. Spoon over boiled new potatoes or sliced fresh tomatoes, or use as a dip for artichokes.
Makes ¾ cup

½ cup mayonnaise or salad dressing
3 tablespoons milk
½ cup watercress leaves (no stems)

Combine all ingredients in an electric-blender container; cover. Beat 1 minute, or until creamy-smooth. (If you do not have an electric blender, chop watercress fine and blend into mayonnaise-milk mixture in a small bowl.)

Pink Zip

Both mayonnaise and sour cream add a special flavor to this topping for cauliflower.
Makes about 1½ cups

¾ cup mayonnaise or salad dressing
¼ cup milk
¼ teaspoon salt
   Dash of cayenne
2 tablespoons catsup
½ teaspoon grated lemon peel
1 tablespoon lemon juice
½ cup dairy sour cream

1 Combine mayonnaise or salad dressing, milk, salt and cayenne in a small saucepan; heat slowly, stirring constantly, just until hot; remove from heat.
2 Stir in catsup, lemon peel and juice, then fold in sour cream slowly. Heat just until warm. (If heated too fast, sauce may separate. If so, quickly stir in a scant tablespoon boiling water.)

Herbed Egg Sauce

Freshly cooked asparagus—and other vegetables, too—go glamorous with this delicate topper.
Makes 3 cups

2 tablespoons chopped onion
4 tablespoons (½ stick) butter or margarine
4 tablespoons all-purpose flour
½ teaspoon salt

¼ teaspoon leaf thyme, crumbled
¼ teaspoon ground ginger
   Dash of pepper
2 cups milk
6 hard-cooked eggs, shelled

1 Sauté onion in butter or margarine until soft in a medium-size saucepan; stir in flour, salt, thyme, ginger and pepper; cook, stirring constantly, just until bubbly. Stir in milk; continue cooking and stirring until sauce thickens and boils 1 minute.
2 Chop eggs coarsely; stir into sauce.
3 Spoon over freshly cooked asparagus, green beans or broccoli.

Chinese Sweet-Sour Sauce

It's a pleasing dressing-seasoner for crisply cooked vegetables.
Makes about 1¼ cups, or enough for 6 cups vegetables

¼ cup firmly packed brown sugar
2 tablespoons cornstarch
½ teaspoon seasoned salt
¾ cup pineapple juice
¼ cup water
2 tablespoons cider vinegar
2 tablespoons honey
2 teaspoons soy sauce

1 Mix brown sugar, cornstarch and seasoned salt in a small saucepan; blend in remaining ingredients. Cook, stirring constantly, until sauce thickens and boils 3 minutes.
2 Pour over crisp-cooked vegetables in a large frying pan; toss to mix well; cover.
3 Simmer 5 to 8 minutes, or just until vegetables are tender.
Note—To prepare and crisp-cook the vegetables, cut scraped carrots into thin pennies, green pepper into thin rings and cabbage into thin shreds. (There should be about 6 cups.) Heat 2 tablespoons vegetable oil in a large frying pan. Add vegetables, tossing to coat with heated oil. Cook, stirring constantly, 2 to 3 minutes, or until vegetables are shiny-moist. Pour sauce over; continue as in Steps 2 and 3.

1727

Polonaise Sauce

Asparagus, cauliflower, broccoli or Brussels sprouts go glamorous with this easy topper.
Makes about ½ cup

SAUCERY

Some plain and fancy saucery: Radish Cream to spoon into oven-hot, fluffy baked potatoes, a skillet full of Chinese Sweet-Sour Sauce, delicious on any crisp-cooked vegetable and a luscious classic Hollandaise.

6 tablespoons (¾ stick) butter or margarine
½ cup coarse soft bread crumbs (1 slice)
1 tablespoon chopped parsley
1 hard-cooked egg, shelled and sieved

1 Melt butter or margarine in a small frying pan; stir in bread crumbs. Heat slowly, stirring often, just until crumbs are lightly toasted. Remove from heat; stir in parsley.
2 Spoon over cooked vegetable; garnish with sieved egg.

Chive-Cheese Sauce
Cheeses are superb for sauce—they melt and blend so beautifully.
Makes about 2¼ cups
  2 tablespoons butter or margarine
  2 tablespoons all-purpose flour
  ½ teaspoon salt
1½ cups milk
  1 package (about 6 ounces) chive cream cheese

1 Melt butter or margarine in a medium-size saucepan; stir in flour and salt; cook, stirring constantly, until bubbly.
2 Stir in milk; continue cooking and stirring until sauce thickens and boils 1 minute.
3 Add cheese; stir in until melted. Serve hot over cooked cabbage.
    PIMIENTO CHEESE SAUCE—Prepare recipe above, substituting 1 jar (about 5 ounces) pimiento cheese spread for chive cream cheese. Serve hot over cooked cauliflower. Makes about 2 cups.
    CARAWAY-CHEESE SAUCE—Prepare recipe above, substituting 3 long slices caraway cheese for chive cream cheese. Serve hot over cooked green beans. Makes about 2 cups.

Olive-Chive Cream
For a different flavor treat, try this continental-style sauce on freshly cooked carrots or broccoli.
Makes 1½ cups

⅓ cup sliced stuffed olives
1 tablespoon drained capers
3 tablespoons butter or margarine
2 teaspoons finely cut chives
1 cup dairy sour cream

1 Sauté olives and capers in butter or margarine, stirring often, 5 minutes in a small heavy saucepan; remove from heat.
2 Stir in chives, then blend in sour cream

1728

slowly. Heat *very slowly*, stirring constantly, just until sour cream is warm.

Radish Cream
Bits of radish give a snappy crunch and peppy flavor to this topper for baked potatoes.
Makes 1¾ cups

1 cup dairy sour cream
1 cup finely chopped radishes (about 1 bunch)
¼ cup finely cut chives
½ teaspoon seasoned salt
¼ teaspoon seasoned pepper

Blend all ingredients in a small bowl; cover. Chill until serving time.

THE SEA'S BOUNTY

THE SEA'S BOUNTY: TIPS ON BUYING FISH AND SHELLFISH; PLAIN AND FANCY FISH RECIPES; FAVORITE SHELLFISH RECIPES

In years past, to enjoy seafood was to live by the sea. To cast out a line and haul in the catch. America's catch was then and is today unusually varied and abundant. From New England's chilly waters comes the magnificent lobster, not to mention cod, haddock, halibut, flounder, clams, oysters and scallops.

The Chesapeake supplies quantities of sweet-meated blue crabs *and* oysters *and* dozens of varieties of food fish. Farther south, in the Carolina Low Country and among Georgia's Golden Isles, there are *more* blue crabs and gorgeously fat, succulent shrimp. The Gulf Coast, however, is America's shrimp capital with a harvest so precious people there call it "pink gold."

The West Coast produces an equally impressive catch: salmon, tuna, Dungeness and Alaska king crabs, exquisite clams and oysters. Inland rivers and lakes, with their treasures of trout, shad, bass, pike and pickerel aren't to be discounted either.

1731

Proof of the sea's bounty (left to right): Scallops Florentine, Cod Provençale, Planked Flounder Fillets.

The beauty of our bounty is that people deep in middle America, miles from either coast, can now enjoy the best of both catches thanks to freezing, canning, rapid packing and shipping (Maine lobsters, for example, are today air-mailed cross country to arrive ferocious and kicking).

In the pages that follow, you will find tips on buying and preparing the most popular fish and shellfish as well as a selection of superb recipes that "do our sea's bounty right proud."

TIPS ON BUYING FISH AND SHELLFISH

Wherever you live, you'll find canned, frozen and fresh fish and seafood the year round to suit every taste and pocketbook. Knowing the different varieties and how to cook them pays off in good eating, easy meal-fixing and—what's best—savings at the checkout counter. Here are more pointers to help you get the most for your money.

On the Grocery Shelves:

Tuna—This favorite shares honors with salmon as tops in popularity among canned seafood items. Because the kind of fish that goes into the can and the price vary, it's good shopping practice to know what you're buying. Two of your best guides are WHITE MEAT and LIGHT MEAT, stamped right on the label. "White meat" simply means Albacore—the whitest, fanciest and most expensive tuna—has been used. "Light meat" tuna is packed from all the other plentiful kinds of fish that are similar in color and flavor, and is an excellent all-purpose

choice. Another factor affecting the price is grade, so look to the label again. "Solid pack" consists of large pieces of choice fish loins and, understandably, costs a little more. "Chunk" tuna, cut in small pieces, carries a moderate price tag, and for the thriftiest buy of all, your dependables are "grated" or "flaked."

Salmon—What would we do without this standby? Here too you'll find a wide range of prices for the familiar 1-pound tall or ½-pound flat tins, depending on the color of the meat. Usually the highest priced salmon has the reddest color, the firmest flakes and is packed in the richest oil. All varieties can be used interchangeably, but some are preferable for salads or cold plates because of their pretty color; others taste just as good in cooked dishes. From highest to lowest in price, they rank like this: Chinook or King; Red or Sockeye; Medium Red or Silver; Pink; Chum or Keta.

Sardines—The most popular come packed in oil or tomato or mustard sauce. And while you have your favorite, of course, it's fun to try something new for a change. Smoked sardines in oil or tomato sauce, foreign packs that are boneless and skinless and those prepared in wines and other fancy sauces are a real treat.

Crab—One of our extra-special shellfish treats, it comes as choice lump meat, flake meat or lump and flake combined. Lump, highest in price, is the choice where color is important. The other two, both thriftier, are excellent for casseroles and creamed dishes or sandwich spreads. Newest comer to the market is "cold-packed" crabmeat. Here the crab is cooked, packed in vacuum tins and shipped in ice. Since it's a refrigerated canned item, most supermarkets stock it in the fish or meat departments.

Other Canned Choices—Among these you'll find shrimps, oysters, clams, lobster, codfish, fish cakes, fish roe and herring. Some are

1732

Almonds and melted butter, exquisite on fish.

Sardines aren't to everyone's taste, but those who relish them do so in a big way. They'll settle for sardines out of the can or in the very simplest sandwiches.

Of all the shellfish that swim along our coast, shrimps are the number one favorite. The best come from the Gulf states.

1733

ready-to-eat, others to heat and eat. And a few to remember for those extra-busy days are creamed tuna, clam chowder, lobster Newburg, oyster stew and seafood cocktail.

In the Freezer Cabinet:

Fish—What a tempting array you'll find here, including pan-ready whole fish, steaks and fillets. Popular choices are cod, sole, haddock, halibut, flounder, perch, catfish, pompano, trout and salmon. Most have no bones, no waste and are excellent buys in both 12-ounce and 1-pound packages. For family-good eating try them pan-fried, broiled or baked, or cook them according to label directions.

Shellfish—Whether you're looking for a family treat or a party fancy, take your pick of lobster tails, shrimps in or out of the shell, green shrimps, oysters, crabs, scallops and clams. Some come in small packages; others, in big family-size bags. New to some areas are frozen oysters individually packed 12 to a tray. Not to be overlooked, too, are those wonderful time-savers—precooked fish, shellfish and seafood dishes that need heating only. Leaders range from frozen complete fish dinners to breaded clams, scallops or shrimps; fish sticks; croquettes; deviled crab or crab cakes; cooked shelled deveined shrimps; and tuna pies or casseroles.

In the Meat Department:

Fresh Fish—Just about every section of the country has its favorite fresh-water or ocean seafoods. And whether it's Boston scrod, Florida red snapper, Great Lakes whitefish, Washington salmon, Colorado trout, California abalone or Maine lobster, all are delicacies. Get to know the specialties in your area, as here is the key to big savings.

QUICK Q AND A ON SEAFOOD

Q. *What is the difference between a fish steak and a fillet?*

A. Steaks are crosswise slices cut from large fish, whereas fillets are sides cut lengthwise from head to tail.

Q. *Should canned fish be drained before using?*

A. This depends mostly on your taste and your recipe. Liquid from tuna or salmon adds to the flavor of stews, chowders, soups, sauces and casseroles. Some homemakers prefer to drain the fish if it is to be used in salads, sandwich fillings or baked loaves, where extra moisture isn't needed.

Q. *How much fish should I buy?*

A. As a rule of thumb, count on ½ to ¾ pound whole fish for each serving. For pan-ready varieties, allow ⅓ to ½ pound.

Q. *What is lox?*

A. It is mild, brine-cured, smoked salmon, most popular for sandwiches and appetizers.

Q. *Is it harmful to eat the bones of canned salmon?*

A. Again it's a personal preference, although many recipes suggest using the liquid and bones, as they are good sources of food minerals and vitamins.

Q. *How many shrimps in a pound?*

A. This will depend on the size—large, medium or small. Usually there will be about 15 of the largest size in a pound, and as many as 60 small ones.

Q. *How can I eliminate fish odors from pans and hands?*

A. After handling fish, wash your hands in hot water and salt, then rinse and wash again with soap. Strong salty water (no soap) takes away the fish odor from dishes and frying pans. Another hint: When poaching shrimps, scallops, or other seafood, try adding ½ teaspoon caraway seeds with other seasonings to the cooking water. They seem to absorb the odor, yet do not change the delicate flavor of the fish.

Q. *What are green shrimps?*

A. They are fresh or raw shrimps that are slightly greenish-gray in color when caught; they turn pink when cooked.

PLAIN AND FANCY FISH RECIPES

Basic Poached Fish

Topped with a Creamy Egg Sauce, this treat rates as a true delicacy. Varieties of fish to poach: halibut or salmon steaks, fresh or frozen flounder, cod or haddock fillets.

⅓ to ½ pound fish fillets per serving
Water
Salt

Onion
Lemon slices
Bay leaf
Peppercorns
CREAMY EGG SAUCE *(recipe follows)*

1 Half-fill a frying pan with water; season with salt, a few onion and lemon slices, bay leaf and peppercorns. Heat to boiling, then turn the heat down low enough to keep water just at simmering.
2 Place fish on a large piece of foil for easy handling; lower into simmering water; cover pan. Simmer 15 minutes for 1-inch-thick steaks. (Watch carefully as overcooking toughens delicate fish).
3 Test for doneness: Stick two forks into thickest part of fish; the "meat" should separate easily into flakes. Lift up foil and remove from pan to drain. Fish is now ready for its sauce.

CREAMY EGG SAUCE—Melt 2 tablespoons butter or margarine in a small saucepan; blend in 2 tablespoons flour and ¾ teaspoon salt; cook, stirring constantly, until bubbly. Stir in 1½ cups milk and 1 teaspoon Worcestershire sauce; cook, stirring constantly, until sauce thickens and boils 1 minute. Stir in 2 hard-cooked eggs, shelled and coarsely chopped. Spoon hot over fish. Makes about 1¾ cups.

Savory Poached Fish
Makes 6 servings

2 packages (12 ounces each) frozen fillets (cod, haddock, flounder, perch or sole)
1 tablespoon vegetable oil
1 small onion, sliced
2 tablespoons lemon juice
1 teaspoon salt
1 teaspoon leaf marjoram, crumbled
¼ teaspoon paprika

1 Remove frozen fish from cartons; let stand at room temperature 15 minutes; cut each block in thirds.
2 Combine oil, onion and seasonings in large frying pan; arrange fish in single layer in pan; add water just to cover fillets; simmer 15 minutes.
3 Lift from pan with slotted spoon; arrange on heated platter; sprinkle with more paprika; serve with TART TARTARE SAUCE.

TART TARTARE SAUCE—Combine ½ cup mayonnaise or salad dressing, 2 tablespoons pickle relish, 1 tablespoon lemon juice and ½ teaspoon Worcestershire sauce in small bowl. Makes ⅔ cup.

Poached Fillets with Shrimp Sauce
Makes 6 servings

2 packages (12 ounces each) frozen fillets of cod, haddock, flounder, perch or sole
1 tablespoon butter or margarine
1 small onion, sliced
2 sprigs of parsley
Handful of celery tops
1 bay leaf
1 teaspoon salt
¼ teaspoon paprika
½ cup milk
1 can frozen cream of shrimp soup
Sliced stuffed olives

1 Remove frozen fish from cartons; let stand at room temperature 15 minutes; cut each block in thirds.
2 Rub a large frying pan with butter or margarine; arrange fish in single layer in pan; add onion, parsley, celery tops, bay leaf, salt and paprika; pour milk around fish.
3 Heat slowly to boiling; cover; simmer gently, basting once or twice with liquid in pan, 15 minutes, or until fish flakes easily.
4 While fish cooks, heat soup in top of double boiler over boiling water; stir in 3 tablespoons milk from poached fish.
5 Arrange fish on heated platter; spoon sauce over; garnish with sliced olives.

Sole Véronique
Makes 4 servings

1 can (10½ ounces) condensed chicken broth
1 soup can of water
⅛ teaspoon salt
Dash of white pepper
⅛ teaspoon bouquet garni for fish
12 seedless green grapes, halved
1 package (1 pound) frozen fillets of sole, thawed
4 tablespoons (½ stick) butter or margarine
4 tablespoons all-purpose flour
2 tablespoons dry white wine

1 Combine chicken broth, water, salt, pepper, bouquet garni and grapes in a large frying pan; heat to boiling.
2 Separate fillets; place in pan; cover. Simmer 12 minutes.
3 Lift fillets from liquid with a pancake turner; place in a shallow baking dish. Pour liquid into a 2-cup measure; add water, if needed, to make 2 cups.
4 Melt butter or margarine in a medium-size saucepan; stir in flour. Cook slowly, stirring constantly, until bubbly. Stir in the 2 cups liquid;

1735

continue cooking and stirring until sauce thickens and boils 1 minute. Stir in wine; pour over fish.

5 Bake in moderate oven (350°) 25 minutes. Serve with cooked rice.

Fillets of Sole in Creole Sauce

Count on a winner here! The fish cooks so flaky-moist in a zippy tomato sauce atop the range.
Makes 6 servings

1 medium-size onion, chopped (½ cup)
½ cup chopped celery
4 tablespoons (½ stick) butter or margarine
1 can (8 ounces) tomato sauce
½ teaspoon salt
½ teaspoon curry powder
⅛ teaspoon pepper
1 cup chopped green pepper
2 packages (1 pound each) frozen fillets of sole, partly thawed

1 Sauté onion and celery in butter or margarine until soft; stir in tomato sauce, salt, curry powder, pepper and green pepper.
2 Cut fish in serving-size pieces; place in a

Sole Véronique is one of the great French classics.

single layer in sauce; cover. Heat to boiling, then simmer 30 minutes, or until fish flakes easily. Serve with cooked rice, if you wish.

Lobster-Stuffed Fillets
Makes 4 servings

½ pound fresh mushrooms*
2 tablespoons butter or margarine
1 to 2 cans (about 6 ounces each) frozen fresh lobster meat, thawed
OR: 1 to 2 cans (about 5 ounces each) lobster meat
4 thin sole or flounder fillets (about 1¼ pounds)
1 cup water
2 thick slices of lemon
1 bay leaf
3 whole cloves
HOLLANDAISE SAUCE (recipe follows)

1 Wash and thinly slice mushroom caps and stems; sauté in butter or margarine in medium-size frying pan about 5 minutes; dice lobster meat (saving a few claw pieces for garnish); heat with mushrooms.
2 Dust fillets lightly with salt and pepper; spoon mushroom-lobster mixture on each; roll up; tie with string. (If fillets are too thick to roll, cut into 8 serving-size pieces; put together with filling, sandwich-style, and fasten with wooden picks to make 4 servings.)
3 Place fish on wire rack in shallow pan containing water, lemon, bay leaf and cloves; cover; simmer 15 to 20 minutes, or until fish flakes easily.
4 Place fish on heated serving plates; cut away strings or remove picks; cover with HOLLANDAISE SAUCE; garnish with lobster claws.

* Or use 1 can (about 3 ounces) sliced mushrooms. Drain liquid into pan for steaming fish.

HOLLANDAISE SAUCE—Melt ¼ cup (½ stick) butter or margarine in top of double boiler; stir in 2 tablespoons hot water; remove from heat. Add 2 unbeaten egg yolks all at once; beat with rotary beater until mixture almost doubles in bulk. Stir in 1 tablespoon lemon juice and a dash each of salt and cayenne. Replace top over hot, *not boiling,* water; cook, stirring constantly, 5 minutes, or until sauce is thick and fluffy-light. (Be sure water in lower part does not touch bottom of top part or boil at any time during cooking.) Remove sauce from heat at once; let stand, uncovered, until ready to serve. Reheat, if necessary, over hot, *not boiling,* water, stirring constantly. Makes about 1 cup.
Note: To make a quick Hollandaise-type sauce, fold ¼ cup dairy sour cream into ½ cup mayonnaise or salad dressing; add 1 tablespoon lemon juice and ½ teaspoon salt.

Baked Roulade of Sole, topped with shrimps and ringed with fresh cooked vegetables: Dramatic dinner in a dish.

Crab-Stuffed Fillets of Sole Roulade with Vegetables

Crab makes the "meaty" stuffing for each moist fish roll served with colorful vegetables and a creamy topper.
Makes 6 servings

1 can (about 7 ounces) crabmeat
6 fresh fillets of sole (about 2 pounds)
 OR: 2 packages (1 pound each) frozen fillets of sole, partly thawed
3 bay leaves
2 teaspoons salt
1 cup water
2 tablespoons lemon juice
6 medium-size carrots, scraped and cut into sticks
2 cups frozen peas (from a 2-pound bag)
3 tablespoons instant-type flour
1 egg
1 lemon, cut into 6 slices

1 Drain liquid from crabmeat into a cup and set aside for making sauce in Step 6. Break crabmeat into large chunks, removing bony tissue, if any.
2 Cut fresh or frozen fillets in half lengthwise. Set aside a few pieces of crabmeat for garnish, if you wish, then place remaining, dividing evenly, on thick end of each fillet; roll up, jelly-roll fashion; fasten with wooden picks. Stand rolls in a medium-size frying pan.
3 Add bay leaves, salt, water and 1 tablespoon of the lemon juice; cover. (Remaining lemon juice is for sauce in Step 7.) Heat to boiling; simmer 15 minutes, or until fish flakes easily.
4 While fish cooks, cook carrot sticks, covered, in boiling lightly salted water in a medium-size saucepan 20 minutes, or until tender; drain; keep hot. Cook peas, following label directions; drain; keep hot.
5 Lift fish rolls from liquid with a slotted spoon; keep hot while making sauce.
6 Pour liquid into a 2-cup measure, discarding bay leaves; add water, if needed, to make 1½ cups. Combine with ¼ cup of the saved crab liquid from Step 1 in a small saucepan; stir in flour; cook, stirring constantly, until sauce thickens and boils 1 minute.
7 Beat egg with remaining 1 tablespoon lemon juice in a small bowl; slowly stir in about 1 cup of the hot sauce, then stir back into remaining in saucepan; remove from heat.
8 When ready to serve, place fish rolls on heated serving plates; spoon carrots and peas around them. Spoon hot sauce over all. Garnish each with saved pieces of crab, a lemon slice and parsley, if you wish.

Baked Roulade of Sole

Fillets are rolled around an herb-seasoned shrimp stuffing, baked and topped with a creamy quick-fix sauce.
Bake at 350° for 30 minutes. Makes 6 servings

3 cups frozen deveined shelled raw shrimps
 (from a 1½-pound bag)

1737

Delicate and delectable Sole and Salmon Roulade.

2 Lay fillets flat on wax paper or foil; spread with shrimp mixture, dividing evenly. Roll up, jelly-roll fashion; fasten with wooden picks.

3 Place, seam side down, in a shallow baking dish. Sprinkle with salt; dot with butter or margarine; drizzle with lemon juice; cover.

4 Bake in moderate oven (350°) 30 minutes, or until fish flakes easily.

5 While fish bakes, prepare MARDI GRAS VEGETABLES. Prepare hollandaise sauce mix, following label directions; keep all warm.

6 Lift fish rolls carefully with a wide spatula and stand on ends in a heated serving dish; remove picks from fish. Spoon MARDI GRAS VEGETABLES in separate piles around edge. Top each fish roll with a saved shrimp; garnish with a cherry tomato cut into eighths almost to bottom and stuffed with a ripe olive, if you wish. Spoon some of the hollandaise sauce over fish; serve remaining separately.

Mardi Gras Vegetables

Cutting vegetables differently gives them an inviting new look.
Makes 6 servings

  6 *large potatoes, pared*
10 *small carrots, pared*
  1 *pound green beans, tipped*
  4 *tablespoons (½ stick) butter or margarine*
  1 *tablespoon chopped parsley*

1 Cut balls from potatoes with a melon-ball cutter or the teaspoon of a measuring-spoon set. (Dice any remaining potatoes to sauté for another meal.)

2 Slice carrots diagonally into ¼-inch-thick slices; cut beans diagonally into 3-inch lengths.

3 Cook vegetables in boiling salted water in separate medium-size saucepans 15 minutes, or just until tender; drain.

4 Season potatoes with 2 tablespoons of the butter or margarine and chopped parsley; season carrots and beans with remaining butter or margarine.

Sole and Salmon Roulade
Makes 8 servings

  1 *fresh salmon steak, weighing about 1 pound*
  4 *fresh fillets of sole, weighing about ½ pound each*
  2 *teaspoons lemon juice*
  ¼ *teaspoon pepper*

1738

  1 *tablespoon shrimp spice*
1½ *cups soft bread crumbs (3 slices)*
  1 *egg, beaten*
  ½ *teaspoon fines herbes*
  6 *fresh fillets of sole (about 2 pounds)*
  ½ *teaspoon salt*
  2 *tablespoons butter or margarine*
  2 *tablespoons lemon juice*
    MARDI GRAS VEGETABLES *(recipe follows)*
  1 *package hollandaise sauce mix*

1 Place shrimps in a 1-inch depth of simmering water seasoned with shrimp spice in a large frying pan; simmer 10 minutes, or just until tender; lift out with a slotted spoon. Set 6 shrimps aside for garnish in Step 6; chop remaining and mix with bread crumbs, egg and fines herbes in a medium-size bowl.

½ cup water
½ cup dry white wine
1 small onion, peeled and sliced
1 teaspoon leaf tarragon
2 egg yolks
½ cup (1 stick) butter or margarine, melted

1 Remove skin and bone from salmon; halve steak crosswise, then cut each half into 4 strips. (Strips may not be quite even, but this won't matter.)
2 Halve each fillet lengthwise; sprinkle with lemon juice and pepper. Place a strip of salmon on thick end of each fillet; roll up, jelly-roll fashion; fasten with wooden picks.
3 Combine water, wine and onion in a medium-size frying pan. Tie tarragon in a small double-thick cheesecloth bag; drop into pan. Stand fish rolls in pan.
4 Heat to boiling; cover. Simmer 5 minutes, or just until fish flakes easily. Lift rolls from liquid with a slotted spoon and place on a deep serving platter; keep warm.
5 Cook liquid in pan rapidly about 3 minutes, or until it measures ½ cup; strain into a cup.
6 Beat egg yolks slightly in the top of a double boiler; stir in about ⅓ of the melted butter or margarine. Place top over simmering, *not boiling,* water. Beat in the ½ cup liquid, alternately with remaining melted butter or margarine; continue beating until mixture is thick and fluffy. Spoon around fish rolls. Garnish each with a tiny sprig of parsley, if you wish.

Baked Fish with Caper Stuffing

Pour the simple milk-butter sauce over frozen fish and chill until baking time.
Bake at 350° for 1 hour and 15 minutes. Makes 6 servings

2 packages (1 pound each) frozen cod or haddock fillets
  Salt and pepper
  Paprika
4 tablespoons (½ stick) butter or margarine
1 cup milk
  CAPER STUFFING (recipe follows)

1 Place frozen blocks of fish in buttered baking dish, 10x6x2; sprinkle lightly with salt, pepper and paprika. Dot with butter or margarine; pour milk around fish. Cover and chill until 1¼ hours before serving time.
2 Bake, uncovered, in moderate oven (350°)

1 hour and 15 minutes, or until fish flakes easily with a fork.
3 Lift fish onto heated serving platter with a slotted wide spatula; cut each block into thirds. Spoon hot CAPER STUFFING on top of each. Or serve the stuffing in a separate bowl, if you wish.

Caper Stuffing

Put it together ahead, then pop into the oven to cook alongside fish.
Bake at 350° for 1 hour. Makes 6 servings

1 large onion, chopped (1 cup)
4 tablespoons (½ stick) butter or margarine
1 cup chopped celery
½ cup chopped parsley
1 tablespoon drained capers
1 teaspoon salt
⅛ teaspoon pepper
½ cup water
6 cups soft bread crumbs (12 slices)

1 Sauté onion in butter or margarine just until soft in large frying pan; add celery, parsley, capers, salt, pepper and water; stir to mix well, then heat to boiling.
2 Add bread crumbs, tossing to mix well. Spoon into a 6-cup baking dish. Cover and chill until 1 hour before serving time.
3 Bake, covered, along with fish in moderate oven (350°) 1 hour, or until crisp and golden at edge.

Baked Orange Fillets of Sole

Orange juice and grated orange rind give this favorite a pleasingly different flavor.
Bake at 350° for 15 minutes for fresh fish, 30 minutes for frozen. Makes 4 servings

4 small fresh fillets of sole (about 1 pound)
  OR: 1 package (1 pound) frozen fillets of sole
1 teaspoon grated orange peel
½ teaspoon salt
⅓ cup orange juice

1 Place fresh fillets in a single layer or block of frozen fish in a shallow baking dish. Sprinkle with orange peel and salt; pour orange juice over.
2 Bake in moderate oven (350°), basting once or twice with juices in pan, 15 minutes, for fresh

Orange juice and rind on fragile white fish—superb!

Stuffed Halibut Steaks
Bake at 350° for 30 minutes. Makes 4 servings

1 cup finely chopped carrots
1 cup finely chopped celery
½ cup thinly sliced green onions
2 tablespoons butter or margarine
1 teaspoon salt
⅛ teaspoon liquid red pepper seasoning
2 tablespoons lemon juice
1 tablespoon chopped parsley
2 packages (about 12 ounces each) frozen halibut steaks, thawed
2 large tomatoes, peeled and quartered
2 large green peppers, halved, seeded and sliced

1 Sauté carrots, celery and green onions in 1 tablespoon of the butter or margarine in a heavy skillet for 5 minutes. Stir in salt, pepper seasoning, 1 tablespoon of the lemon juice and parsley.
2 Melt remaining tablespoon of butter or margarine; brush small amount over bottom of a shallow baking dish; place halibut steak from one package in bottom of dish (if there is more than one piece in package, fit pieces tightly together); top with vegetable mixture, then with halibut from second package.
3 Run metal skewers vertically through both layers of fish and stuffing to hold in place. Add tomatoes and peppers. Blend remaining lemon juice with remaining melted butter or margarine; brush some over surface of halibut; sprinkle with remaining salt.
4 Bake in moderate oven (350°) 30 minutes, brushing occasionally with lemon-butter mixture, or until halibut flakes easily.

fish, 30 minutes for frozen, or until fish flakes easily with a fork.
3 Place on heated serving platter; garnish with an orange slice and parsley, if you wish.

Baked Orange Halibut Steaks
Bake at 350° for 30 minutes. Makes 4 servings

1740

2 packages (about 12 ounces each) frozen halibut steaks
¼ teaspoon salt
¼ teaspoon grated orange peel
½ cup orange juice
2 tablespoons chopped parsley

1 Place frozen halibut steaks in a single layer in a shallow baking dish. Sprinkle with salt and orange peel; pour orange juice into baking dish.
2 Bake in moderate oven (350°), basting once or twice with juices in dish, 30 minutes, or until fish flakes easily.
3 Place on a heated serving platter; sprinkle with parsley.

Broiled Paprika Halibut
It's hard to find an easier or more attractive way to cook fish. Paprika adds a rosy glow.
Makes 6 servings

6 halibut steaks, each cut about ¾ inch thick and weighing about 6 ounces
3 tablespoons butter or margarine, melted
Paprika
Salt and pepper
CUCUMBERS VINAIGRETTE (recipe follows)
1 lemon, cut in wedges
Parsley

1 Place halibut steaks in single layer on buttered broiler pan; brush with about half the

Few fish dishes are simpler to make or more satisfying to eat than fork-tender Broiled Paprika Halibut.

melted butter or margarine; sprinkle with paprika, salt and pepper.

2 Broil, about 6 inches from heat, 10 to 12 minutes; turn; brush with remaining butter or margarine, then sprinkle again with paprika, salt and pepper. Broil 10 to 12 minutes longer, or until lightly golden and fish flakes easily with a fork.

3 Lift onto heated serving platter; garnish with CUCUMBERS VINAIGRETTE, lemon wedges, and parsley. Serve with tartare sauce, if you wish.

Cucumbers Vinaigrette

Each slice is crisp and crunchy with a pleasing vinegary zip.
Makes 6 servings.

Score the rind of 1 medium-size cucumber with a fork; slice thin into medium-size bowl. (There will be about 2 cups.) Sprinkle with ½ teaspoon salt and ⅛ teaspoon pepper; spoon 2 tablespoons cider vinegar and 2 tablespoons water over; toss to mix well. Chill. Drain before serving.

Planked Flounder Fillets

Bake at 400° for 15 minutes. Makes 6 servings.

2 packages (1 pound each) frozen flounder fillets, thawed
¼ cup (½ stick) butter or margarine
2 tablespoons lemon juice
½ teaspoon paprika
  RICH DUCHESS POTATOES (recipe follows)
1 package (10 ounces) frozen mixed vegetables, cooked, drained, and seasoned
  BUTTERY CHERRY TOMATOES (recipe follows)
  Watercress

1 Separate fish fillets carefully; arrange in a single layer on a cookie sheet.

2 Melt butter or margarine in a small saucepan; stir in lemon juice and paprika. Brush part of mixture on fish fillets.

3 Broil fillets about 4 inches from heat, 5 minutes.

4 Transfer fillets from cookie sheet with wide spatula, layering in the center of a seasoned 15x10-inch plank (see note), or a flameproof platter.

5 Fill a pastry bag with RICH DUCHESS POTATOES; pipe 6 nests of potatoes around the plank; border plank between nests with remaining potatoes. Brush remaining paprika-butter on fish.

6 Bake in hot oven (400°) 15 minutes, or until potatoes are tipped with golden brown. At serving time, fill potato nests with seasoned mixed vegetables. Garnish plank with BUTTERY CHERRY TOMATOES and watercress.

Note—To season a new plank, rub it well with vegetable oil on top and sides; heat on rack in very slow oven (275°) 1 hour; cool; wipe off any excess oil.

Rich Duchess Potatoes

Makes 6 servings

6 medium-size potatoes, pared
⅓ cup milk
2 eggs
2 tablespoons butter or margarine
1 teaspoon salt

1 Cook potatoes in boiling salted water 15 minutes, or until tender in a large saucepan; drain. Return potatoes to pan and shake over low heat until dry and fluffy.

2 Mash potatoes; beat in milk, eggs, butter or margarine and salt until fluffy-light. Cool.

BUTTERY CHERRY TOMATOES—Remove stems from 1 cup cherry tomatoes. Melt 2 tablespoons butter or margarine in a small skillet. Sauté tomatoes over low heat, stirring gently, just until skins burst. Sprinkle with 1 tablespoon chopped parsley.

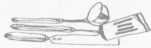

Golden-Crisp Fish Fillets

Heat about ¼-inch depth vegetable shortening or oil in large frying pan; add frozen fish-fillet squares (cod, haddock, perch or flounder—packed 6 to a 14-ounce package); fry, following label directions, 3 to 4 minutes on each side, or until cooked through and golden. Drain quickly on paper towels; serve with CUCUMBER DIP. Makes 6 servings.

CUCUMBER DIP—Pare 1 small cucumber; quarter lengthwise; discard seeds; chop pulp coarsely. Stir into ½ cup dairy sour cream in small bowl; season with 2 tablespoons liquid from a jar of dill pickles, ½ teaspoon salt and a dash of cayenne; top with a sprinkling of freshly ground pepper. Makes about ¾ cup.

Captain's Seafood Platter

Bake at 375° for 25 minutes.
Makes 6 servings

1 package (1 pound) frozen breaded fish sticks

1 package (7 ounces) frozen deviled crab miniatures
1 package (1 pound) frozen French fried potatoes
Vegetable shortening or oil for frying
2 packages (10 ounces each) frozen peas,
cooked, drained and seasoned
FRESH TARTARE SAUCE (recipe follows)
BRIGHT SEAFOOD DIP (recipe follows)

1 Arrange frozen fish sticks on a large cookie
sheet (be sure to leave room for crab miniatures).
2 Bake in moderate oven (375°) 10 minutes;
add crab miniatures and bake 15 minutes
longer.
3 Cook French fries in shortening for frying,
following label directions, in a large skillet; drain
on paper toweling and keep hot.
4 Arrange fish sticks, crab miniatures and fried
potatoes in mounds on a heated serving platter.
Spoon peas into a bowl and place on same
platter. Spoon FRESH TARTARE SAUCE and BRIGHT
SEAFOOD DIP into two small bowls; place on
platter. Garnish with wedges of lemon and watercress or parsley, if you wish.

Fresh Tartare Sauce
Makes about ¾ cup

½ cup mayonnaise or salad dressing
¼ cup chopped sweet pickles
2 tablespoons chopped green onions
Few drops liquid red pepper seasoning

Combine all ingredients in a small bowl; cover;
chill at least 1 hour to blend flavors

Bright Seafood Dip
Makes about ¾ cup

½ cup chili sauce
2 tablespoons chopped parsley
1 tablespoon prepared horseradish
1 tablespoon lemon juice
Combine all ingredients in a small bowl; cover;
chill at least 1 hour to blend flavors.

Friday Cod Cakes
Fish and potatoes share honors in these crusty
golden pan-fried patties.
Makes 6 servings

1 package (4 ounces) dried shredded codfish

4 medium-size potatoes, pared and quartered
(about 1½ pounds)
2 tablespoons butter or margarine
¼ teaspoon pepper
1 egg
3 tablespoons vegetable shortening

1 Place codfish in a strainer lined with cheesecloth; rinse under running cold water for 1 minute; drain well.
2 Cook potatoes in boiling salted water in medium-size saucepan 15 minutes, or until tender.
Drain, then mash or put through ricer into a
medium-size bowl. Beat in butter or margarine
and pepper; stir in egg and codfish.
3 Shape into 12 even-size patties; sauté in vegetable shortening in large frying pan 10 minutes on each side, or until richly browned.

Cod Provençale
Makes 4 servings

1 large onion, chopped (1 cup)
1 clove of garlic, minced
3 tablespoons olive oil or vegetable oil
2 large ripe tomatoes
1 teaspoon salt
1 teaspoon leaf thyme, crumbled
¼ teaspoon pepper
1 package (1 pound) frozen cod fillets (not
thawed)
Boiled potatoes
Cucumber slices
Chopped parsley

1 Sauté onion and garlic in olive oil or vegetable
oil until soft in a large skillet with a cover.
2 Peel, core and chop tomatoes; stir into onion
mixture and cook 2 minutes; add salt, thyme
and pepper.
3 Place frozen fish block in the sauce in skillet,
spooning part of the sauce over fish; cover
skillet.
4 Simmer 20 minutes, or until fish flakes easily
with a fork. Transfer fish with a wide spatula
to a heated serving platter; spoon sauce over
and around fish. Surround with boiled potatoes
and cucumber slices; garnish with chopped
parsley.

1743

Fisherman's Pie
Bake at 350° for 35 to 40 minutes.
Makes 6 servings

¼ cup milk
¼ cup (½ stick) butter or margarine
1 cup soft bread crumbs (2 slices)
1 package (1 pound) frozen cod fillets, thawed
3 egg yolks, lightly beaten
2 tablespoons chopped parsley
1 tablespoon lemon juice
1 tablespoon grated onion
½ teaspoon Worcestershire sauce
½ teaspoon salt
⅛ teaspoon pepper
3 egg whites, stiffly beaten

1 Heat milk and butter or margarine slowly in medium-size saucepan until butter melts; stir in bread crumbs; let stand 5 minutes.
2 Flake cod into crumb mixture; slowly stir in egg yolks, then parsley, lemon juice, onion, Worcestershire sauce, salt and pepper; mix well; fold in beaten egg whites.
3 Spoon into buttered 6-cup shallow baking dish; place in pan with 1-inch depth of hot water.
4 Bake in moderate oven (350°) 35 to 40 minutes, or until firm.
5 Spoon or cut in pie-shape wedges; serve with EGG-CAPER SAUCE.

Egg-Caper Sauce
Makes about 1½ cups

2 tablespoons butter or margarine
2 tablespoons all-purpose flour
¼ teaspoon salt
⅛ teaspoon pepper
1¼ cups milk
1 tablespoon capers, drained
2 hard-cooked eggs, coarsely chopped

1 Melt butter or margarine in top of small double boiler; remove from heat; blend in flour, salt and pepper; slowly stir in milk; cook over low heat, stirring constantly, until mixture thickens and boils 1 minute.
2 Stir in capers and eggs; place over hot water to keep hot until serving time.

1744

Caribbean Fish Stew
Makes 8 generous servings

2 packages (1 pound each) frozen fish fillets (cod, haddock, flounder or perch)
4 medium-size potatoes, pared and diced (about 4 cups)
1 large sweet onion, sliced

1 tablespoon sugar
2 teaspoons salt
¼ teaspoon pepper
1 tablespoon Worcestershire sauce
1 teaspoon mixed pickling spice (tied in cheesecloth bag)
3 cans (about 1 pound each) tomatoes
1 fresh lime
2 tablespoons butter or margarine

1 Let fish fillets stand at room temperature to thaw partly while preparing Step 2.
2 Combine potatoes, onion, sugar, salt, pepper, Worcestershire sauce, pickling spice in bag and tomatoes in large kettle; heat to boiling; cover; reduce heat; simmer about 30 minutes, or just until potatoes are tender.
3 Cut fish fillets into 1-inch cubes with sharp knife; add to potato mixture; cover; cook 12 to 15 minutes, or just until fish flakes easily; remove spice bag.
4 Ladle into serving tureen; stir in juice from half the lime; top with butter or margarine and garnish with the other half of lime, sliced.

Fishermen's Stew
Makes about 8 cups

4 slices bacon, cut into 1-inch pieces
1 large onion, chopped
3 cups diced potatoes
2 teaspoons sugar
1 teaspoon salt
¼ teaspoon leaf thyme, crumbled
1 bay leaf
⅛ teaspoon pepper
4 tomatoes, peeled and quartered
2 cups water
1 package (1 pound) frozen fish fillets
  Chowder crackers

1 Fry bacon pieces in kettle until crisp; remove and save for topping; add onion and potatoes; sauté, stirring often, until onions are golden; stir in seasonings, tomatoes and water; cover.
2 Simmer over low heat about 25 minutes; add block of frozen fish; continue cooking 20 minutes longer, or until fish flakes easily.
3 Divide fish carefully into 4 servings; ladle with liquid into big bowls, top with crisp bacon pieces; serve with chowder crackers.

Ceviche

Good as an appetizer or salad.
Makes 6 to 8 servings

3 pounds halibut
1 cup lime juice
1 can (1 pound) tomatoes
1 jar (3 ounces) pimiento-stuffed olives, drained
1 large onion, chopped (1 cup)
½ cup catsup
½ cup olive oil
2 teaspoons salt
1 teaspoon leaf oregano crumbled
1 teaspoon liquid red pepper seasoning
1 firm ripe avocado

1 Trim skin and bones from halibut; cut halibut into ½-inch cubes; place in a deep glass or pottery bowl. Pour lime juice over top. (There should be enough to cover fish.) Cover bowl; chill overnight.
2 Drain halibut; rinse under cold water; place in a large bowl.
3 Break up any large pieces of tomato; add tomatoes and juice, olives, onion, catsup, olive oil, salt, oregano and red pepper seasoning to bowl; toss lightly to mix.
4 Just before serving, halve avocado; pit, peel and dice. Spoon halibut mixture into a serving bowl; scatter avocado around edge.

SOME FAVORITE SALMON RECIPES

Poached Salmon Steaks

Makes 4 servings

1 large lemon, cut in 6 slices
2 slices onion
1 bay leaf
½ teaspoon salt
3 peppercorns
4 salmon steaks, each cut 1-inch thick
1 jar (5 ounces) hollandaise sauce

1 Half fill a large frying pan with water; season with 2 of the lemon slices, onion, bay leaf, salt and peppercorns; heat to boiling.
2 Place salmon steaks in pan; cover. Simmer 15 minutes, or until fish flakes easily with a fork; drain.
3 While salmon cooks, heat hollandaise sauce, following label directions.
4 Place salmon steaks on serving plates; spoon hollandaise sauce over each. Garnish with remaining lemon slices.

Baked Salmon Steaks

Our flavor secret is borrowed from a famous French seaside specialty called matelôte.
Bake at 350° for 30 minutes. Makes 6 servings

6 salmon steaks, cut ½ inch thick
1 envelope Italian-salad-dressing mix
½ cup water
2 tablespoons lemon juice
1 can (3 or 4 ounces) sliced mushrooms

1 Arrange salmon steaks in single layer in buttered baking dish, 13x9x2. Combine salad-dressing mix, water and lemon juice in 1-cup measure; pour over salmon; cover.
2 Bake in moderate oven (350°) 15 minutes; uncover; pour mushrooms and liquid over; baste fish with liquid in dish.

Salmon Florentine

Makes 4 servings

1 package (about 10 ounces) spinach
1 can (1 pound) pink salmon
3 tablespoons butter or margarine
3 tablespoons all-purpose flour
½ teaspoon salt
½ teaspoon dillweed
1½ cups milk
1 egg, beaten
2 tablespoons lemon juice

1 Trim stems and any coarse leaves from spinach. Wash leaves well; place in a large saucepan; cover. (There's no need to add any water.)
2 Cook 1 minute over low heat, or just until spinach wilts; drain well; chop.
3 Drain salmon; remove skin and bones; break into small pieces.
4 Melt butter or margarine in a small saucepan; stir in flour, salt and dillweed. Cook, stirring constantly, just until bubbly. Stir in milk; continue cooking and stirring until sauce thickens and bubbles 1 minute. Stir half of hot mixture into beaten egg in a small bowl; return to saucepan; cook, stirring constantly, 1 minute, or until sauce thickens again.
5 Fold 1 cup of the hot sauce into salmon. Line 4 scallop shells or 4 individual foil baking dishes with chopped spinach. Spoon salmon mixture onto center of spinach. Spoon remaining hot sauce over salmon.
6 Broil, about 4 inches from heat, 3 minutes, or until tops are light brown and bubbly. Garnish with a slice of lemon and a sprig of parsley, if you wish.

Albert Stockli's* Fresh Salmon Steak Baked in Red Wine with Grapes
Bake at 400° for 15 minutes. Makes 4 servings

4 salmon steaks, 8 to 10 ounces each
1 teaspoon salt
¼ teaspoon pepper
1 tablespoon butter or margarine, melted
3 tablespoons shallots (or onion), finely chopped
½ cup dry red wine
Juice of ½ lemon
½ teaspoon cornstarch dissolved in 1 tablespoon cold water
½ cup seedless green grapes

1 Butter an ovenproof baking dish large enough to hold the 4 salmon steaks. Season the steaks with salt and pepper and brush with the melted butter or margarine. Place in oven (400°) 5 minutes.
2 In the meantime, prepare the sauce by combining the shallots, red wine and lemon juice in a small saucepan. Bring to a boil and simmer over medium heat for 5 minutes. Stir in the dissolved cornstarch to thicken sauce. Pour sauce over fish.
3 Return to the oven for 10 minutes. Add the grapes during the last 5 minutes of baking time and serve hot.

* Albert Stockli's credentials are fabulous. Born in Switzerland, he is the former chef of New York's renowned Four Seasons restaurant and the present owner of the Stonehenge Inn in Ridgefield, Connecticut, one of the finest eating places in the country. He is also a commandeur of the Commanderie des Cordons Bleus and Maître de Cuisine & Chevaliers of the Confrèries des Chevaliers du Tastevin. But even with this prestigious background, Stockli has an amazingly simple approach to fine cooking, as his salmon steak recipe proves.

*"SPLENDID FARE" BY ALBERT STOCKLI. COPYRIGHT © 1970 BY ALBERT STOCKLI. REPRINTED BY PERMISSION OF ALFRED A. KNOPF, INC.

Salmon Loaf with Easy Dill Sauce
"Scrumptious" best describes this seafood dish with its creamy herb topper.
Bake at 350° for 40 minutes. Makes 6 servings

1 can (1 pound) salmon
4 tablespoons butter or margarine
¼ cup milk
1 cup coarsely crumbled soda crackers (12 crackers)
3 eggs, separated
2 tablespoons chopped parsley
1 tablespoon grated onion
1 tablespoon lemon juice
½ teaspoon Worcestershire sauce
½ teaspoon salt
⅛ teaspoon pepper
EASY DILL SAUCE (recipe follows)

1 Grease a loaf pan, 9x5x3; line bottom and ends with a strip of wax paper, leaving a 1-inch overhang; grease paper.
2 Drain liquid from salmon into medium-size saucepan; stir in butter or margarine and milk; heat until butter is melted. Stir in crackers; let stand 5 minutes.
3 Flake salmon, removing large bones and skin; fold into crumb mixture. Beat egg yolks; blend into salmon mixture with parsley, onion, lemon juice, Worcestershire sauce, salt and pepper.
4 Beat egg whites just until they form soft peaks in medium-size bowl; fold into salmon mixture. Pour into pan.
5 Set in shallow baking pan; place on oven shelf; pour in boiling water to depth of 1 inch.
6 Bake in moderate oven (350°) 40 minutes, or until thin-blade knife inserted in center comes out clean.
7 Remove pan from water at once; let stand 5 minutes. Loosen loaf from sides of pan with knife, then lift up ends of paper to loosen, and unmold onto heated platter; peel off wax paper. Slice and serve with EASY DILL SAUCE.

EASY DILL SAUCE—Melt 2 tablespoons butter or margarine over low heat in medium-size saucepan. Stir in 2 tablespoons all-purpose flour, 1 teaspoon dillweed, ½ teaspoon salt, ⅛ teaspoon pepper; cook, stirring all the time, just until mixture bubbles. Stir in 1½ cups milk slowly; continue cooking and stirring until sauce thickens and boils 1 minute. Makes 1½ cups.

1747

Salmon Swiss Pie
Bake at 450° for 15 minutes; then at 325° for 30 minutes. Makes one 9-inch pie

1 can (about 8 ounces) salmon
2 cups (½ pound) grated natural Swiss cheese

Fresh, tender salmon steaks baked in shallot-scented red wine sauce, Albert Stockli's luscious creation.

2 teaspoons grated onion
1 tablespoon all-purpose flour
¼ teaspoon salt
1 unbaked 9-inch PASTRY SHELL (recipe follows)
3 eggs
1 cup milk

1 Drain salmon; remove any skin or small bones; flake fish.
2 Combine cheese, onion, flour and salt in medium-size bowl; fill pastry shell with alternate layers of salmon and cheese mixture.
3 Beat eggs and milk in large measuring cup or medium-size bowl; pour over salmon-cheese layers in pastry shell.
4 Bake in very hot oven (450°) 15 minutes; reduce heat to slow (325°); bake 30 minutes longer, or just until firm in center.

Pastry Shell
Makes one 9-inch shell

1½ cups sifted all-purpose flour
½ teaspoon salt
½ cup vegetable shortening
About 3 tablespoons cold water

1 Sift flour and salt into medium-size bowl.
2 Cut in shortening with pastry blender or 2 knives until mixture is crumbly.
3 Sprinkle water over mixture, tossing lightly with fork until dough just holds together; press into ball.
4 Roll out dough to an 11-inch round on lightly floured pastry cloth or board.
5 Line 9-inch pie plate with pastry; trim edge, allowing ½-inch overhang; turn overhang under, folding flush with rim of pie plate; flute edge.

1748

Ribbon Salmon Bake
Creamy baked-on topping sparked with chives doubles as a sauce for this softly set loaf.
Bake at 375° for 25 minutes. Makes 6 to 8 servings

2 cans (1 pound each) salmon, drained, boned and flaked
2 cans (10½ ounces each) condensed cream of potato soup
1 small onion, grated

½ cup coarse soft bread crumbs (1 slice)
1 cup (8-ounce carton) dairy sour cream
2 tablespoons cut chives

1 Combine salmon, soup, onion and bread crumbs in a medium-size bowl; toss lightly to mix. Spoon into a greased baking pan, 9x9x2.
2 Spoon sour cream in rows over salmon mixture; sprinkle with chives.
3 Bake in moderate oven (375°) 25 minutes, or until bubbly-hot. Mark into serving-size blocks; lift out with a pancake turner.

Baked Salmon Puffs
Bake at 300° for 45 to 50 minutes. Makes 4 servings

1 can (1 pound) salmon
3 eggs, separated
¾ cup (about 1½ slices) bread crumbs
1 tablespoon finely chopped onion
1 tablespoon lemon juice
½ teaspoon salt
⅛ teaspoon pepper
OLIVE SAUCE (recipe follows)

1 Drain salmon; remove any skin or small bones; flake fish.
2 Beat egg whites in medium-size bowl until stiff but not dry.
3 Beat egg yolks slightly in second medium-size bowl; add salmon, bread crumbs, onion, lemon juice, salt and pepper; mix well; fold in beaten egg whites.
4 Spoon mixture into 4 lightly greased 6-ounce custard cups.
5 Place custard cups in deep baking pan; pour boiling water into pan to depth of 1 inch.
6 Bake in slow oven (300°) 45 to 50 minutes, or until knife inserted in center of puffs comes out clean.
7 Serve with OLIVE SAUCE.

OLIVE SAUCE—1 cup dairy sour cream and ¼ cup sliced stuffed olives in small bowl.

Salmon Supper Mold
Freshly cooked salmon steak is the star of this fluffy main-dish salad.
Makes 6 servings

1 fresh or frozen salmon steak (about ¾ pound)
4 peppercorns

1 teaspoon salt
1 slice of lemon
1 slice of onion
    Handful of celery leaves
    Water
1 envelope unflavored gelatin
1 envelope instant vegetable broth
1½ cups water
1 teaspoon grated onion
1 teaspoon lemon juice
⅛ teaspoon pepper
    OR: Few drops liquid red pepper seasoning
½ cup mayonnaise or salad dressing
1 cup chopped celery

1 Simmer salmon steak with peppercorns, ½ teaspoon salt, lemon and onion slices and celery leaves in just enough water to cover in a medium-size frying pan, 15 minutes, or until salmon flakes easily with a fork.
2 Lift out carefully with a slotted spatula; drain on paper toweling until cool enough to handle, then remove skin and bones. Flake salmon; place in a small bowl. (There should be about 1½ cups.) Set aside for Step 4.
3 Soften gelatin with vegetable broth in 1 cup of the water in a medium-size saucepan; heat, stirring constantly, just until gelatin dissolves. Stir in remaining ½ cup water, onion, lemon juice, remaining ½ teaspoon salt, pepper or red pepper seasoning. Chill 30 to 40 minutes, or until as thick as unbeaten egg white.
4 Stir in mayonnaise or salad dressing; fold in salmon and celery. Spoon into a 4-cup mold; chill several hours, or until firm.
5 Just before serving, run a sharp-tip thin-blade knife around top of mold, then dip mold *very quickly* in and out of a pan of hot water. Invert onto serving plate; carefully lift off mold. Serve with lemon wedges to squeeze over, or with your favorite bottled tartare sauce, if you wish.

Senegalese Salmon Salad
Makes 6 servings

1 package (6 ounces) curry-flavor rice mix
    Butter or margarine
    Water
1 can (1 pound) salmon
1 cup diced celery
¼ cup sliced stuffed olives
2 teaspoons grated lemon peel
¼ cup cream for whipping
½ cup mayonnaise or salad dressing
    Iceberg lettuce

1 Prepare rice mix with butter or margarine and water, following label directions. Place in a large bowl; cool, then cover and chill about an hour.
2 While rice chills, drain liquid from salmon; remove skin and bones. Flake salmon; fold into rice mixture with celery, olives and lemon peel.
3 Beat cream until stiff in a small bowl; fold in mayonnaise or salad dressing; fold into salmon mixture.
4 Place lettuce leaves on serving plates to form cups; spoon salmon mixture into cups. Garnish with sliced olives.

Party Salmon Platter
Fancy molded salad is its company star to frame with zippy-seasoned vegetables.
Makes 6 to 8 servings

GLAZED SALMON MOLD (recipe follows)
2 medium-size yellow squashes
1 package (10 ounces) frozen Fordhook lima beans
1 can (1 pound) sliced beets, drained
1 envelope onion salad-dressing mix
    Cider vinegar
    Vegetable oil
1 head Boston lettuce, separated into leaves

1 Prepare GLAZED SALMON MOLD and chill.
2 Wash yellow squashes; trim ends, then quarter each lengthwise; cut in 2-inch sticks. Cook, covered, in a small amount of boiling salted water in a medium-size frying pan 20 minutes, or until crisply tender; drain.
3 Cook lima beans, following label directions; drain. Place squashes, beans, and beets in separate shallow dishes.
4 Prepare salad-dressing mix with vinegar, water, and salad oil, following label directions. Drizzle part over each vegetable; cover. Chill at least an hour to season and blend flavors.
5 When ready to arrange platter, place GLAZED SALMON MOLD in the center of a large platter. Arrange lettuce cups around edge; fill with seasoned vegetables. Garnish with sprigs of fresh dill, onion rings, pimiento strips and dill-pickle slices, if you wish.

1749

Glazed Salmon Mold
Makes 6 to 8 servings

1 can (1 pound) salmon
1 can (about 7 ounces) crabmeat

THE SEA'S BOUNTY

Glazed Tuna-Salmon Mold, decorated here with thinly sliced radishes and green pepper slivers instead of with sliced water chestnuts and strips of pimiento.

2 hard-cooked eggs, shelled and chopped
1 cup finely diced celery
¾ cup mayonnaise or salad dressing
1 tablespoon lemon juice
1 teaspoon grated onion
¼ teaspoon freshly ground pepper
1 envelope unflavored gelatin
1 envelope instant vegetable broth
  OR: 1 vegetable bouillon cube
2 cups water
  Few drops liquid red pepper seasoning
10 radishes, sliced thin
¼ small green pepper, cut in thin strips
1 slice stuffed olive

1 Drain salmon; flake finely, removing any dark bits of skin. Drain crabmeat; flake and remove bony tissue, if any. Combine both with chopped eggs and celery in a large bowl.

2 Blend in mayonnaise or salad dressing, lemon juice, onion and pepper. Spoon into a 6-cup fish-shape mold, packing down well with back of spoon; cover. Chill at least an hour.

3 While mold chills, soften gelatin with vegetable broth or bouillon cube in water in a small saucepan. Heat, stirring constantly and crushing cube, if using, with a spoon, just until gelatin dissolves; remove from heat. Stir in liquid red pepper seasoning; cool at room temperature. (For a slightly pink color, stir in 1 teaspoon beet liquid from can.)

4 Unmold salmon mold by running a sharp-tip thin-blade knife around top to loosen; invert into a jelly-roll pan; lift off mold.

5 Measure ⅔ cup of the cooled gelatin mixture into a small bowl; place in a larger bowl partly filled with ice and water. Chill, stirring several times, 2 to 3 minutes, or until as thick as unbeaten egg white. Spoon over salmon mold to make a layer. Chill until gelatin is firm.

6 Arrange sliced radishes on top of gelatin for fish "scales," pepper strips for "tail" and "fins," and olive slice for "eye."

7 Chill another ⅔ cup gelatin mixture, following Step 5; carefully spoon over decorations on top of mold. Chill again until firm. Chill remaining gelatin; spoon over top to make a thick coating, then chill mold at least 4 hours, or until very firm. (Overnight is even better.)

8 When ready to serve, trim away any excess gelatin around bottom of mold. Lift mold onto a large serving platter with two wide spatulas or pancake turners.

1750

SOME FAVORITE TUNA RECIPES

Deviled Tuna Bake

Fancy French seafood en coquille inspired this recipe for an inviting casserole.
Bake at 350° for 20 minutes. Makes 4 servings

    2 tablespoons butter or margarine
    2 tablespoons all-purpose flour
    1 teaspoon dry mustard
    ½ teaspoon salt
 1½ cups milk
    ¼ teaspoon liquid red pepper seasoning
    1 tablespoon lemon juice
    1 can (about 7 ounces) tuna, drained and
      flaked
    ¾ cup coarsely crumbled soda crackers (9
      crackers)
    4 hard-cooked eggs, shelled
      Parsley

1 Melt butter or margarine in medium-size saucepan; remove from heat; blend in flour, mustard and salt; slowly stir in milk. Cook, stirring constantly, until sauce thickens and boils 1 minute.
2 Stir in liquid red pepper seasoning, lemon juice, tuna and ½ cup cracker crumbs. (Save remaining crumbs and 1 egg for topping and garnish.)
3 Chop remaining 3 eggs coarsely; stir into tuna mixture; pour into buttered shallow 4-cup baking dish or 9-inch pie plate. Sprinkle saved ¼ cup cracker crumbs over top.
4 Bake in moderate oven (350°) 20 minutes, or until crumbs are golden. Quarter saved egg lengthwise; arrange on casserole to form a petal design; center with a sprig of parsley.

1752

Dixie Tuna

Bake at 350° for 30 minutes. Makes 4 to 6 servings

    2 cans (15 ounces each) macaroni and cheese
    2 cans (about 7 ounces each) tuna, drained
      and flaked
    ½ cup thinly sliced celery
    1 cup packaged corn-bread stuffing mix (from
      an 8-ounce package)

1 Combine macaroni and cheese, tuna and celery in a buttered 6-cup baking dish; stir lightly to mix. Sprinkle stuffing mix over top.

2 Bake in moderate oven (350°) 30 minutes, or until bubbly and topping is lightly toasted.

Tuna-Rice Bake

Bake at 350° for 30 minutes. Makes 4 to 6 servings

    1 can (10¾ ounces) condensed cream of ve-
      getable soup
    1 small can evaporated milk (⅔ cup)
    ⅔ cup water
    ¼ cup chopped parsley
    4 cups cooked rice
    2 cans (about 7 ounces each) tuna, drained
      and flaked
    1 jar (2 ounces) sliced pimientos
    1 cup coarsely broken cheese crackers

1 Combine soup, milk and water in a small saucepan; heat to boiling. Stir in parsley.
2 Spoon half of the rice into a buttered 6-cup baking dish; top with half each of the tuna, pimientos and soup mixture. Repeat layers with remaining rice, tuna, pimientos and soup mixture. Sprinkle cheese crackers around edge.
3 Bake in moderate oven (350°) 30 minutes, or until bubbly and crackers are toasted. Garnish with parsley, if you wish.

Tuna-Pepper Casserole

Makes 4 servings

    2 medium-size green peppers
    1 can (about 7 ounces) tuna, drained and
      flaked
    1 can (10½ ounces) condensed cream of
      mushroom soup
    ¼ cup milk
    3 tablespoons chopped pimientos
    3 tablespoons chopped stuffed green olives
    3 tablespoons prepared tartare sauce
    4 slices American cheese, halved diagonally
    ½ cup buttered bread crumbs

1 Halve peppers and scoop out seeds. Place peppers in a large frying pan; pour in boiling water to a depth of ½ inch; cover. Cook 15 minutes; drain. Slice peppers into ½-inch-wide strips; place in a 6-cup shallow baking dish.
2 Mix tuna with soup, milk, pimientos, olives and tartare sauce in a medium-size bowl; spoon half over pepper strips; top with half of the

Deviled Tuna Bake inspired by two classics: French Coquilles St. Jacques and our own deviled blue crab. ➤

cheese. Repeat with remaining tuna mixture and cheese; sprinkle with buttered crumbs.
3 Bake in moderate oven (350°) 25 minutes, or until bubbly.

Tuna-Potato Pie

Bake at 375° for 55 minutes. Makes 6 servings

    1 package piecrust mix
    3 medium-size potatoes
    2 large onions
    1 can (about 7 ounces) tuna
    6 tablespoons (¾ stick) butter or margarine
    1½ teaspoons salt
    ¼ teaspoon pepper
    3 tablespoons chopped parsley
      Milk

1 Prepare piecrust mix, following label directions, or make pastry from your favorite two-crust recipe. Roll out half the pastry to a 12-inch round on a lightly floured pastry cloth or board; fit into a 9-inch pie plate; trim overhang to ½ inch.
2 Pare potatoes and cut into *very thin* slices; peel onions and cut into thin slices; drain and flake tuna.
3 Layer potatoes, onions and tuna in shell, dotting each layer with part of the butter or margarine and sprinkling with part of the salt, pepper and parsley.
4 Roll out remaining pastry to an 11-inch round; cut slits near center to let steam escape; cover pie. Trim overhang to ½ inch; turn edges under, flush with rim; flute to make a stand-up edge. Brush pastry with milk. Sprinkle with sesame seeds, if you wish.
5 Bake in moderate oven (375°) 55 minutes, or until potatoes are tender and pastry is golden. Cool at least 10 minutes before serving.

Tuna Biscuit Bake

Bake at 400° for 20 minutes. Makes 5 servings

    3 tablespoons butter or margarine
    1 medium-size onion, chopped (½ cup)
    1 medium-size stalk of celery, chopped
    3 tablespoons all-purpose flour
    ½ teaspoon salt
    ⅛ teaspoon curry powder
      Dash of pepper
    2 cups milk
    1 can (about 7 ounces) tuna, drained and
      flaked
    1 can (about 8 ounces) peas, drained
    3 tablespoons chopped dill pickle
    1 package refrigerated biscuits

1 Melt butter or margarine in medium-size saucepan; add onion and celery; sauté 10 minutes, or just until tender; remove from heat.
2 Blend in flour, salt, curry powder and pepper; slowly stir in milk.
3 Cook over low heat, stirring constantly, until sauce thickens and boils 1 minute.
4 Stir in tuna, peas and dill pickle; heat to boiling, stirring often.
5 Pour into 1½-quart baking dish; arrange biscuits on top.
6 Bake in hot oven (400°) 20 minutes, or until biscuits are golden-brown.

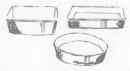

Tuna Soufflé

Bake at 325° 45 to 50 minutes. Makes 4 servings

    3 tablespoons butter or margarine
    3 tablespoons all-purpose flour
    ½ teaspoon salt
      Dash of pepper
    1 cup milk
    2 teaspoons finely minced onion
    ⅛ teaspoon leaf marjoram, crumbled
    ½ teaspoon Worcestershire sauce
    ½ teaspoon lemon juice
    4 eggs, separated
    1 can (about 7 ounces) tuna, drained and
      flaked

1 Melt butter or margarine in small saucepan; remove from heat.
2 Blend in flour, salt and pepper; slowly stir in milk.
3 Cook over low heat, stirring constantly, until sauce thickens and boils 1 minute; stir in onion, marjoram, Worcestershire sauce and lemon juice; cool sauce slightly.
4 Beat egg whites in medium-size bowl until stiff but not dry. (Do not overbeat.)
5 Beat egg yolks in large bowl until thick and lemon-colored; blend in cooled sauce; gently fold in flaked fish and beaten egg whites.
6 Pour mixture into ungreased 1½-quart baking dish.
7 Bake in slow oven (325°) 45 to 50 minutes, or until center is firm when lightly pressed with fingertip. Serve at once.

Tuna Soufflé Pie

The golden meringue topping is a piquant soufflé sauce.
Bake at 400° about 40 minutes. Makes 4 to 6 servings

1 nine-inch unbaked pastry shell
2 cans (about 7 ounces each) tuna
2 eggs, separated
¾ cup milk
1 small onion, grated
2 tablespoons chopped parsley
½ teaspoon salt
⅛ teaspoon pepper
½ cup mayonnaise
2 tablespoons sweet-pickle relish
1 tablespoon lemon juice
    Dash of cayenne

1 Prepare 9-inch pastry shell with packaged piecrust mix or use your own favorite recipe.
2 Drain tuna; flake in medium-size bowl; beat egg yolks with milk in small bowl (save egg whites for topping in Step 4); stir into tuna with onion, parsley, salt and pepper; spoon into pastry shell.
3 Bake in hot oven (400°) 30 minutes, or just until firm on top.
4 Beat egg whites in small bowl; fold in mayonnaise, pickle relish, lemon juice and cayenne; spread on top of pie; bake 10 minutes longer, or until puffed and golden.
5 Cut into wedges and serve at once.

Tuna Coquilles
Bake at 375° for 8 to 10 minutes. Makes 6 servings

3 tablespoons butter or margarine
¼ cup diced green pepper
2 tablespoons minced onion
3 tablespoons all-purpose flour
¼ teaspoon salt
⅛ teaspoon pepper
⅛ teaspoon leaf marjoram, crumbled
1¼ cups milk
1 can (3 or 4 ounces) sliced mushrooms
1 teaspoon Worcestershire sauce
2 cans (about 7 ounces each) tuna, flaked
1 teaspoon sherry
¾ cup (about 1½ slices) buttered coarse bread crumbs
¼ cup grated Cheddar cheese

1 Melt butter or margarine in medium-size saucepan; add green pepper and onion; sauté 5 minutes, or just until tender.
2 Blend in flour, salt pepper and marjoram; slowly stir in milk, mushrooms and liquid and Worcestershire sauce.
3 Cook, stirring constantly, until mixture thickens and boils 1 minute.
4 Stir in tuna and sherry; heat until bubbly.

5 Spoon hot mixture into 6 scallop shells or ramekins (½-cup size).
6 Combine buttered bread crumbs and Cheddar cheese; sprinkle over tuna mixture.
7 Bake in moderate oven (375°) 8 to 10 minutes, or until golden-brown and bubbly-hot.

Tuna Ramekins
Bake at 400° for 15 minutes. Makes 4 servings

1 can (about 7 ounces) tuna
1 pimiento, chopped
½ cup soft bread crumbs (1 slice)
1 can (10½ ounces) cream of celery soup
¼ cup milk
1 cup canned peas, drained
1 package refrigerated biscuits

1 Drain tuna; break into small pieces into medium-size bowl; add pimiento, bread crumbs, soup, milk and peas; mix well; spoon into ramekins.
2 Flatten 4 biscuits; cut out centers with small biscuit cutter; place rings on top of tuna mixture; arrange remaining biscuits and centers in greased cake pan.
3 Bake ramekins and biscuits in hot oven (400°) 15 minutes, or until biscuits are golden. Decorate biscuits on top of ramekins with pimiento bows, if you wish.

Golden Flake Tuna Loaf
The men on our taste panel gave this unusual dish a 5-star rating. Do try it and see how it scores with your family.
Bake at 375° for 45 minutes. Makes 6 servings

1 small onion, chopped (¼ cup)
4 tablespoons (½ stick) butter or margarine
½ cup milk
1½ cups soft bread crumbs (3 slices)
2 cans (about 7 ounces each) tuna, drained and flaked
1 can (about 1 pound) sauerkraut, drained and chopped
2 eggs
1 tablespoon lemon juice
½ teaspoon salt
¼ teaspoon pepper
    SAVORY EGG SAUCE (recipe follows)

1 Sauté onion in butter or margarine just until softened in small saucepan; stir in milk; heat to boiling; remove from heat. Beat in bread crumbs until mixture is thick and well blended.
2 Mix remaining ingredients, except SAVORY EGG SAUCE, with bread mixture in large bowl; pack into well-greased loaf pan, 9x5x3.

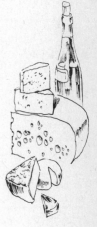

3 Bake in moderate oven (375°) 45 minutes, or until firm in center and browned around edges. Let stand in pan about 5 minutes, then turn out onto heated serving platter. (Loaf will be soft, so handle carefully.) Slice with sharp knife and serve with SAVORY EGG SAUCE.

SAVORY EGG SAUCE—Sauté 1 tablespoon minced onion in 3 tablespoons butter or margarine just until softened in medium-size saucepan; remove from heat. Blend in 3 tablespoons all-purpose flour, ½ teaspoon salt, and ¼ teaspoon pepper; stir in 1½ cups milk. Cook, stirring constantly, until sauce thickens and boils 1 minute. Fold in 2 hard-cooked eggs, shelled and diced; 1 pimiento, diced; and 1 tablespoon chopped parsley. Makes about 2 cups.

Tunaburgers
Bake at 400° about 15 minutes. Makes 4 servings

    1 can (7 ounces) tuna, drained and flaked
    1 cup (4 ounces) cubed Swiss cheese
    ½ cup cubed cooked potatoes
    ⅓ cup chopped celery
    2 radishes, thinly sliced
    1 tablespoon chopped parsley
    1 teaspoon grated onion
    ⅛ teaspoon curry powder
    ⅓ cup mayonnaise or salad dressing
    4 round rolls, split and buttered

1 Combine tuna, Swiss cheese, potatoes, celery, radishes, parsley, onion, curry powder and mayonnaise or salad dressing in medium-size bowl; stir lightly until well mixed; divide evenly among buttered rolls; wrap each roll in aluminum foil.
2 Bake in hot oven (400°) 15 minutes, or until heated through and cheese is melted.

1756

Supper Tuna Bowl
Makes 6 servings

    1 package (½ pound) medium noodles
    2 tablespoons butter or margarine
    2 tablespoons all-purpose flour
    ¼ teaspoon salt
    ⅛ teaspoon pepper
    2 teaspoons grated orange peel
    ½ teaspoon grated lemon peel
    1¼ cups milk
    2 tablespoons orange juice

    2 cans (about 7 ounces each) tuna, drained
      and broken into bite-size pieces

1 Cook noodles until tender in large amount of salted water in large saucepan; drain; return to saucepan; add butter or margarine.
2 Blend in flour, salt, pepper, orange and lemon peels; stir in milk and orange juice.
3 Cook over low heat, stirring constantly, until mixture boils 1 minute; add tuna; heat until bubbly.
4 Spoon into heated serving dish; garnish with orange slices and watercress, if desired.

Seaside Success
Here's popular tuna salad with a skillet twist. Chinese noodles and shredded lettuce are the crisp extras.
Makes 6 servings

    1 envelope instant vegetable broth
      OR: 1 vegetable-bouillon cube
    1 teaspoon instant minced onion
    ½ cup diced celery
    ½ cup water
    2 cans (about 7 ounces each) tuna, drained
      and flaked
    4 hard-cooked eggs, shelled and coarsely
      chopped
    ½ cup mayonnaise or salad dressing
    ¼ cup sliced stuffed green olives
    1 tablespoon chopped parsley
    2 teaspoons lemon juice
    1 small head iceberg lettuce, washed and
      shredded
    1 can (3 ounces) Chinese fried noodles

1 Combine vegetable broth or bouillon cube, onion, celery and water in a medium-size frying pan; cover. Heat to boiling; simmer 5 minutes.
2 Add tuna and eggs; cover. Heat just until bubbly-hot; remove from heat.
3 Blend mayonnaise or salad dressing, olives, parsley and lemon juice in a cup; spoon over tuna mixture. Toss lightly to mix; push to one side.
4 Place shredded lettuce in a pile in pan; sprinkle noodles over tuna. Serve warm right from the skillet.

Molded Tuna Loaf
Makes 6 to 8 servings

    2 envelopes unflavored gelatin
    1 cup cold water

2 cups hot water
½ cup lemon juice
½ cup sugar
¼ teaspoon salt (for gelatin mixture)
2 cans (about 7 ounces each) tuna, drained and flaked
1 cup diced celery
¼ cup finely chopped pimiento
1 tablespoon prepared horseradish
¼ cup cider vinegar
2 tablespoons vegetable oil
½ teaspoon salt (for tuna mixture)
¼ teaspoon paprika
Dash of pepper

1 Soften gelatin in cold water in medium-size bowl; add hot water; stir until gelatin dissolves.
2 Stir in lemon juice, sugar and ¼ teaspoon salt; chill until syrupy.
3 While gelatin chills, combine flaked tuna, celery, pimiento and horseradish in medium-size bowl; mix vinegar, salad oil, ½ teaspoon salt, paprika and pepper in cup; pour over fish mixture and toss lightly; let stand 30 minutes.
4 Fold syrupy gelatin mixture into fish mixture; spoon into loaf pan, 9x5x3*; chill several hours, or until firm.
5 Unmold on serving platter; garnish with curly endive and tomato wedges or cherry tomatoes, if desired.

* To make fancy decorated top: Before chilling gelatin mixture, pour a thin layer into bottom of loaf pan; chill until firm (keep remaining gelatin mixture at room temperature). Make a design on firm gelatin layer of thinly sliced olives and cherry-tomato halves or pimiento circles; carefully spoon over enough cool gelatin mixture just to cover design; chill until firm. Finish making mold as directed in Step 4.

Glazed Tuna-Salmon Mold
This gourmet specialty takes a bit of fussing, but it's really easy to make.
Makes 6 to 8 servings

2 cans (about 7 ounces each) tuna, drained and finely flaked
2 cans (about 8 ounces each) salmon, drained and finely flaked
2 hard-cooked eggs, shelled and sieved
1 cup finely diced celery
1 can (about 5 ounces) water chestnuts, drained
2 tablespoons chopped parsley
1 teaspoon grated onion
1 cup mayonnaise or salad dressing

1 tablespoon lemon juice
½ teaspoon prepared mustard
Few drops liquid red pepper seasoning
2 envelopes unflavored gelatin
1 envelope instant chicken broth
1 teaspoon salt
2 cups water
½ small onion, sliced thin
2 cups ice and water
1 slice stuffed olive
1 pimiento, cut in thin strips

1 Combine tuna, salmon, sieved eggs and celery in a large bowl.
2 Slice 8 water chestnuts very thin and set aside in a cup for making fish "scales" in Step 7. Chop remaining very fine and stir into salmon mixture with parsley and onion.
3 Blend mayonnaise or salad dressing, lemon juice, mustard and liquid red pepper seasoning in a 2-cup measure; fold into salmon mixture. Spoon into a 6-cup fish-shape mold, packing down well with back of spoon; cover. Chill at least 2 hours.
4 While salmon chills, soften gelatin with chicken broth and salt in the 2 cups water in a small saucepan; add onion. Heat slowly, stirring constantly, until gelatin dissolves. Strain over ice and water in a 4-cup measure, stirring until ice melts.
5 Pour 2 cups gelatin mixture into a shallow pan, 9x9x2; chill 2 hours, or until firm, to use for garnish in Step 8. Let remaining gelatin stand at room temperature 15 minutes, or just until as thick as unbeaten egg white.
6 While gelatin stands, unmold fish this way: Run a sharp-tip thin-blade knife around top to loosen; invert onto large serving platter; lift off mold.
7 Spoon a thin layer of slightly thickened gelatin from Step 5 over molded fish to coat completely. (Some of the gelatin will run off into platter, making a base for garnish in Step 8.) Set olive slice in place for "eye," strips of pimiento for "mouth," "tail" and "fins" and sliced water chestnuts for "scales." Carefully spoon another layer of gelatin over top. Chill a few minutes, or until sticky-firm, then spoon on any remaining thickened gelatin to make a smooth coating. Chill until serving time.
8 Just before serving, cut gelatin in pan into small squares; spoon around mold on platter. Garnish with lemon wedges dipped in chopped parsley, if you wish.

1757

Some of America's seafood favorites on the half shell: Scallops, clams, shrimps and rosy rock lobster tails.

SOME FAVORITE SHELLFISH RECIPES

Crab and Tuna Ring with Curried Peas

Two favorites, delicately seasoned, bake in a ring mold. For pretty serving, turn out and set a small bowl of creamy peas in center.
Bake at 350° for 45 minutes. Makes 6 servings

4 slices white bread, cut in ½-inch cubes
1 can (3 or 4 ounces) chopped mushrooms
¾ cup milk
1 can (about 7 ounces) crabmeat
1 can (about 7 ounces) tuna
1 egg
2 tablespoons chopped parsley
CURRIED PEAS (recipe follows)

1 Combine bread cubes, mushrooms and liquid and milk in a small saucepan; heat slowly just until milk is hot.
2 Drain crabmeat; flake and remove parsley in a medium-size bowl; toss lightly to mix well. Beat milk mixture, then blend in. Spoon into a well-greased 3-cup ring mold.
3 Bake in moderate oven (350°) 45 minutes, or until top is firm and golden brown.
4 Let stand 5 to 10 minutes; loosen around edge with knife; invert onto heated serving platter; lift off mold. Serve with CURRIED PEAS.

Curried Peas

Slide them into the oven first, as they take a bit longer to cook than the seafood mold.
Bake at 350° for 1 hour. Makes 6 servings

1 package (10 ounces) frozen green peas
1 medium-size onion, peeled
1 large lettuce leaf
2 tablespoons butter or margarine
½ teaspoon curry powder
1 can (10½ ounces) condensed cream of mushroom soup

1 Place peas in a 4-cup baking dish; grate onion over top; then cover with lettuce leaf.
2 Bake in moderate oven (350°) 45 minutes, or just until tender.
3 Remove lettuce; mix in butter or margarine and curry powder, then stir in soup; return to oven. Bake 15 minutes longer, or until sauce is bubbly-hot in center.

1758

Crab and Shrimp Supreme

Bake at 300° about 30 minutes. Makes 4 servings

1 can (about 7 ounces) king crabmeat, drained, boned and coarsely flaked
1 can (about 5 ounces) shrimps, drained
2 tablespoons bottled Italian-style salad dressing
1 can (10 ounces) frozen cream of shrimp soup
1 cup cream for whipping
1 cup coarsely chopped watercress
½ cup buttered soft bread crumbs
2 tablespoons grated Parmesan cheese
½ teaspoon paprika

1 Marinate crabmeat and shrimps in salad dressing about 1 hour.
2 Heat soup and cream in medium-size saucepan over low heat, stirring often, until soup melts; stir in crab-shrimp mixture.
3 Layer with chopped watercress into four 1-cup baking dishes; top with mixture of bread crumbs. Parmesan cheese and paprika.
4 Bake in slow oven (300°) about 30 minutes, or until bubbly-hot.

Crab Pilaf

Similar to fried rice, with crab as the meat. Rice sautés best if cooked the day before.
Makes 4 to 6 servings

1 can (about 7 ounces) crabmeat
6 tablespoons vegetable oil
1 small onion, sliced
½ cup diced celery
1 package (10 ounces) frozen mixed vegetables, thawed
3 cups cold well-drained cooked rice (about ¾ cup uncooked)
¼ cup salted peanuts
Soy sauce

1 Drain crabmeat; flake and remove bony tissue, if needed.
2 Heat 4 tablespoons of the vegetable oil in a large frying pan; stir in onion, celery and mixed vegetables. Sauté, stirring several times, 15 minutes, or until vegetables are crisply tender. Remove and set aside for Step 4.
3 Stir remaining 2 tablespoons vegetable oil and cooked rice into same pan; cook, stirring often, over medium heat 10 minutes, or just until rice grains separate and turn creamy-white.
4 Stir in crabmeat, sautéed vegetables and peanuts. Heat, stirring once or twice, just until hot. Spoon into a heated bowl; serve with soy sauce to drizzle over.

Creamy Crab Parisienne

Makes 6 servings

2 packages (10 ounces each) frozen broccoli spears
1 package onion-sauce mix
1 egg, separated
2 cans (about 7 ounces each) crabmeat drained and flaked

Creamy Crab Parisienne, an "instant" classic made of frozen broccoli, canned crab, onion-sauce mix.

1 teaspoon lemon juice
¼ cup mayonnaise or salad dressing

1 Cook broccoli, following label directions; drain. For individual servings, divide among 6 broilerproof shallow serving dishes. Or layer into 1 six-cup shallow dish.

2. While broccoli cooks, prepare onion-sauce mix, following label directions; beat into egg yolk gradually in a medium-size bowl; fold in crabmeat and lemon juice.

3 Beat egg white until it forms soft peaks in a small bowl; fold in mayonnaise or salad dressing.

4 Spoon hot crab mixture over broccoli in each dish, dividing evenly, then top with mayonnaise mixture.

5 Broil, about 4 inches from heat, 5 minutes, or until sauce puffs and turns golden. Serve at once.

Seafood Mandalay
Makes 4 servings

4 tablespoons (½ stick) butter or margarine
4 tablespoons all-purpose flour
1 teaspoon curry powder
1 envelope instant vegetable broth
*   OR: 1 vegetable-bouillon cube*
2 cups buttermilk
1 can (about 7 ounces) crabmeat, drained
1 can (about 5 ounces) deveined shrimps, drained and rinsed
1 can (about 1 pound) peas and onions, drained
1⅓ cups packaged precooked rice
½ teaspoon salt
*   Boiling water*

1 Melt butter or margarine in a medium-size saucepan; stir in flour, curry powder and vegetable broth or bouillon cube. Cook, stirring constantly, just until bubbly; remove from heat.

2 Stir in buttermilk. Cook slowly, stirring constantly, until sauce thickens and boils 1 minute.

3 Fold in crab, shrimps and peas and onions, heat very slowly just until hot.

4 Prepare rice with salt and boiling water, following label directions. Spoon into a shallow serving dish. Spoon curry mixture on top. Serve with bottled chutney, sliced green onions or slivered almonds to sprinkle on top, if you wish.

Double-Boiler Crab Soufflé
It puffs beautifully and holds up well, even if dinnertime is delayed.
Makes 4 servings

1 can (about 7 ounces) crabmeat
1 teaspoon grated onion
⅛ teaspoon curry powder
2 tablespoons butter or margarine
2 tablespoons all-purpose flour
½ teaspoon salt
⅔ cup milk
1 tablespoon chopped parsley
4 eggs, separated

1 Drain crabmeat and flake, removing bony tissue, if any.

2 Sauté onion with curry powder in butter or margarine 1 minute in a small saucepan; stir in flour and salt; cook, stirring constantly, just until bubbly. Stir in milk; continue cooking and stirring until sauce thickens and boils 1 minute; remove from heat. Stir in flaked crabmeat and parsley; let cool while beating eggs.

3 Beat egg whites until they form soft peaks in a medium-size bowl.

4 Beat egg yolks until creamy-thick in a second medium-size bowl; blend in cooled crab sauce; fold in beaten egg whites until no streaks of white remain. Pour into the top of an ungreased 8-cup double boiler; place over simmering water; cover.

5 Cook, keeping water simmering all the time, 1 hour and 5 minutes, or until soufflé is firm on top. Serve at once. (If soufflé must stand, cover and keep hot over simmering water.)

Crab Newburg
Bake at 350° for 1 hour and 20 minutes. Makes 8 servings

2 cans (about 7 ounces each) crab meat
2 packages (10 ounces each) frozen peas
2 cans (10½ ounces each) condensed cream of mushroom soup
¼ cup dry sherry
1 can (6 ounces) sliced mushrooms, drained
1 can or jar (4 ounces) pimientos, drained and diced
3 slices white bread, cut in tiny cubes
3 tablespoons butter or margarine, melted

1 Drain crabmeat; remove bony tissue, if any; break crab into bite-size chunks.

2 Cook peas, following label directions; drain.

3 Blend mushroom soup and sherry until smooth in a small bowl.

4 Layer half of the crabmeat, peas, mushrooms and pimientos into a 10-cup refrigerator-to-oven baking dish; repeat layers. Pour soup mixture over top. Cover; chill.

1760

Crêpes (French pancakes) need not be served as Suzettes or dessert. Try rich Crab and Shrimp Crêpes.

5 About 1½ hours before serving time, toss bread cubes with butter or margarine in a small bowl; sprinkle over mixture in baking dish. Do not cover.
6 Bake 1 hour and 20 minutes, or until bubbly in center and crumb topping is toasted.

Crab and Shrimp Crêpes
Makes 14 to 16 appetizer servings

Crêpes
Makes about 3½ dozen appetizer crêpes or eight 8-inch crêpes

¾ *cup sifted all-purpose flour*
1 *tablespoon sugar*
½ *teaspoon salt*
3 *eggs*
1 *cup milk*
1 *tablespoon melted butter or margarine*

1 Measure flour, sugar and salt into sifter.
2 Beat eggs just until blended in a large bowl; sift flour mixture over top and beat in just until smooth; stir in milk and melted butter or margarine.

For appetizer crêpes:
3 Heat a griddle slowly; test temperature by sprinkling on a few drops of water. When drops bounce about, temperature is right. Grease griddle lightly with butter or margarine.
4 Measure batter, a scant tablespoon at a time, onto griddle; spread into a 3-inch round with back of spoon.
5 Bake 1 minute, or until tops are set and undersides are golden; turn. Bake 1 minute longer, or until bottoms brown. As crêpes are baked, roll up, jelly-roll fashion, and place on a cookie sheet; keep warm. Repeat with remaining batter, lightly greasing griddle before each baking.

For 8-inch crêpes:
3 Heat an 8-inch heavy frying pan and grease lightly the same as in Step 3 above.
4 Measure batter, a scant ⅓ cup at a time, into pan, tilting pan to cover bottom completely.
5 Bake 1 to 2 minutes, or until tops are set and undersides are golden; turn. Bake 1 to 2 minutes longer, or until bottoms brown. As crêpes are baked, roll up, jelly-roll fashion and place on a cookie sheet; keep warm. Repeat with remaining batter, greasing pan before each baking.
6 Fill baked crêpes with CRAB AND SHRIMP SAUCE.

1761

Crab and Shrimp Sauce

1 can (about 7 ounces) crabmeat
1 can (5 ounces) deveined shrimps
3 tablespoons butter or margarine
3 tablespoons all-purpose flour
½ teaspoon salt
Dash of cayenne
1½ cups milk
1 egg yolk
1 tablespoon golden dry sherry
2 tablespoons light cream or table cream

1 Drain crabmeat, removing bony tissue, if any; flake into a medium-size bowl. Drain shrimps; rinse; chop. Combine with crabmeat.
2 Melt butter or margarine in a medium-size saucepan; stir in flour, salt and cayenne; cook, stirring constantly, until bubbly. Stir in milk; continue cooking and stirring until sauce thickens and boils 1 minute; remove from heat.
3 Beat egg yolk slightly in a small bowl; stir in sherry and cream. Slowly stir in a generous ½ cup of the hot sauce, then stir back to remaining sauce in pan. Cook slowly, stirring constantly, 1 minute. Fold ⅓ cup into crab mixture; keep remaining sauce warm.
4 Unroll crêpes, one at a time; place a teaspoon of crab mixture on each; reroll. Place in a single layer in a large chafing dish or keep-hot server; spoon remaining sauce around crêpes. Serve hot.
Note—If your chafing dish is not large enough to hold all of the filled crêpes, place half each of the crêpes and sauce in dish at a time.

California Appetizer Tray
Nestle sliced lobster, crab in tiny cups and artichoke hearts in ice so they'll stay chilled during serving.
Makes 8 servings

1 small head of salad bowl or butter (Boston) lettuce
½ cup ripe olives, drained
½ cup green olives, drained
2 jars (6 ounces each) marinated artichoke hearts, drained
SLICED ROCK LOBSTER (recipe follows)
DILLED FLAKED CRAB (recipe follows)

1 Trim core close to head of lettuce; wash under running cold water; drain well. Gently pull leaves apart to resemble a flower; set in center of large serving tray lined with crushed ice.
2 Tuck ripe and green olives among leaves; surround with marinated artichoke hearts, SLICED ROCK LOBSTER, and tiny individual serving cups of DILLED FLAKED CRAB.

SLICED ROCK LOBSTER—Cook 4 frozen small South African lobster tails (they come 3 or 4 to a 10-ounce package) with half a lemon, sliced, 1 teaspoon mixed whole spices and ½ teaspoon salt, following label directions. Drain and cool completely. With scissors, cut through and remove the thick membrane on underside of shell. Take out lobster meat by peeling hard shell back with fingers of one hand and pulling meat toward you with the other. Cut meat into ½-inch-thick slices, keeping slices in order. Sprinkle with lemon juice; lay back in shell. Wrap each in wax paper, foil or transparent wrap; chill until serving time.

DILLED FLAKED CRAB—Thaw 1 package (6 ounces) frozen king crabmeat. (Or use 1 can [7 ounces] king crabmeat, drained, or 6 ounces freshly cooked crabmeat.) Flake into small pieces; place in a small bowl. Drizzle with 2 teaspoons vegetable oil and 2 teaspoons cider vinegar; sprinkle ¼ teaspoon salt and ¼ teaspoon dillweed over; toss lightly to mix. Chill at least an hour to blend flavors. Spoon into 8 tiny serving cups or individual salt dishes.

King Crab Salad Bowls
Makes 6 servings

¾ cup mayonnaise or salad dressing
¼ cup chili sauce
2 tablespoons lemon juice
¼ cup sliced green onions
2 tablespoons finely chopped parsley
2 cans (about 8 ounces each) king crabmeat
4 slices processed white American cheese
2 firm ripe avocados
1 small head iceberg lettuce
¼ cup toasted sliced almonds

1 Blend mayonnaise or salad dressing, chili sauce, lemon juice, green onions and parsley in a small bowl; chill at least a half hour to season.
2 Pick over crabmeat, removing bony tissue, if any; flake crab. Cut cheese into julienne strips. Halve avocados; peel, pit and dice.
3 Shred lettuce; divide among 6 individual salad bowls. Place crabmeat, cheese strips and avocados in rows over lettuce; sprinkle with almonds. Pass dressing separately to spoon on top.

A Chef's Salad can be made with seafood as well as with meat. This one features sumptuous king crab.

Seafood Chef's Salad
Makes 4 servings

 1 head Boston or leaf lettuce
 1 can (7 ounces) king crabmeat
 2 hard-cooked eggs, shelled
10 radishes
    MARINATED SCALLOPS (recipe follows)
    CARROT CURLS (recipe follows)
 1 cup cottage cheese
    Paprika
    TOMATO DRESSING (recipe follows)

1 Line a large salad bowl with lettuce leaves; break up remaining lettuce into bite-size pieces into bowl.
2 Drain and pick over crabmeat, removing any bits of bone but keeping meat in big chunks. Quarter eggs lengthwise. Wash and slice radishes.
3 Arrange in mounds with MARINATED SCALLOPS and CARROT CURLS in a ring on lettuce. Fill center with cottage cheese; dust with paprika. Serve with TOMATO DRESSING.

Marinated Scallops
Makes 4 servings

½ pound (about 20) sea scallops
   OR: 1 package (7 ounces) frozen sea scallops
 2 cups water
 1 slice of onion
 1 slice of lemon
 2 peppercorns
 3 tablespoons TOMATO DRESSING (recipe follows)

1 Wash fresh scallops under cold running water; drain. (Keep frozen scallops in iced block.)

2 Heat water, onion, lemon and peppercorns to boiling in medium-size saucepan; simmer 5 minutes. Add scallops; cover; simmer 5 minutes (7 to 10 minutes, if frozen).
3 Remove with slotted spoon; drain well; place in shallow dish. Spoon TOMATO DRESSING over to marinate; cover; chill.

Carrot Curls
Chilly ice-water bath makes these crisp strips curl neatly.
Scrape and halve 2 carrots lengthwise. Shave into long paper-thin strips with vegetable parer. Roll each strip around finger; slide off into a bowl of ice water; let stand to curl.

Tomato Dressing
Count just 3 calories for each tablespoonful of this zippy dressing.
Makes about 1¼ cups

1 envelope French-dressing mix
¾ cup tomato juice
¼ cup cider vinegar
2 tablespoons water

Combine all ingredients in 2-cup jar with screw top; shake well; chill. Shake again just before using.

Patio Crab Salad with Louis-Dressing Mold
Delicately flavored crabmeat is complemented with fresh pineapple, dill and a tangy cheese-dressing mold.
Makes 6 servings

3 packages (about 6 ounces each) frozen king crabmeat, thawed
2 tablespoons lemon juice
1 small ripe pineapple
  LOUIS-DRESSING MOLDS (recipe follows)
  Romaine
  Fresh dill
6 lemon wedges

1 Drain and pick over crabmeat, removing any bits of bone but keeping meat in big chunks; place in medium-size bowl; sprinkle evenly with lemon juice; cover; chill.
2 Cut 6 thin slices from pineapple; cut away skin and "eyes," then cut each slice into 3 fan-shape pieces; snip off core from tip of each fan.
3 Arrange 3 pineapple pieces in fan shape, a mound of crabmeat and a LOUIS-DRESSING MOLD

on romaine in individual salad bowls; garnish with fronds of dill and a lemon wedge; serve with chopped dill to sprinkle over, if you like.

Louisiana Crab Salad
Makes 4 to 6 servings

3 cups warm cooked rice
2 tablespoons bottled Italian-style salad dressing
1 can (about 5 ounces) crabmeat, drained and flaked
1 cup finely diced celery
2 diced pimientos
2 tablespoons lemon juice
1 tablespoon chopped fresh dill
1 teaspoon grated onion
¼ teaspoon salt
¼ cup mayonnaise or salad dressing
  Salad greens

1 Marinate rice with salad dressing in medium-size bowl; let stand at room temperature about 1 hour, then chill.
2 Combine crabmeat, celery, pimientos, lemon juice, dill, onion and salt in second bowl; cover; chill.
3 To serve, combine rice and crabmeat mixture; fold in mayonnaise or salad dressing; serve on crisp salad greens; garnish with sprigs of dill, if you wish.

Louis-Dressing Molds
Makes 6 molds

1 envelope unflavored gelatin
¼ cup cold water
½ cup hot water
2 teaspoons sugar
2 tablespoons lemon juice
1 cup mayonnaise
¼ cup chili sauce
½ cup cream for whipping
½ cup crumbled blue cheese

1 Soften gelatin in cold water in small bowl; add hot water and sugar; stir until dissolved; add lemon juice.
2 Beat in mayonnaise and chili sauce until creamy-smooth; stir in cream and blue cheese.
3 Pour into six 4-ounce molds or custard cups; chill until firm; unmold and serve with PATIO CRAB SALAD.

Crab-Fruit Bowl

Big chunks of crab, plus tangy fruits and artichokes, make this summery selection.
Makes 8 servings

2 packages (6 ounces each) frozen king crabmeat
    OR: 2 cans (about 7 ounces each) king crabmeat
1 head of leaf lettuce
1 can (1 pound, 4 ounces) pineapple slices, drained
1 can (about 1 pound) grapefruit sections, drained
1 avocado, halved, pitted, peeled and sliced
1 cup coconut chips (from a 5-ounce can)
1 jar (6 ounces) marinated artichoke hearts, drained
2 slices of lime
    PINK LIME DRESSING (recipe follows)

1 Thaw frozen crabmeat; cut into chunks, removing any bony tissue. (If using canned crabmeat, drain first.)
2 Line a large shallow salad bowl with lettuce leaves; break remaining leaves into bite-size pieces into bowl.
3 Place crabmeat, pineapple slices, grapefruit sections, avocado slices, coconut chips and artichoke hearts in separate piles on top.
4 Garnish crabmeat with lime slices. Serve with PINK LIME DRESSING.
    PINK LIME DRESSING—Blend ½ cup mayonnaise or salad dressing, 2 tablespoons chili sauce, ½ teaspoon ground ginger and 1 tablespoon lime juice in a 1-cup measure; chill. Makes ¾ cup.

Basic Cooked Shrimps

Pamper shrimps with short, gentle simmering, as this is the secret of tender delicacy every time. It doesn't matter whether you shell shrimps before or after cooking, but they'll take up more flavor from seasonings if shelled first.

6 medium-size shrimps per serving
    Water
    Lemon slices
    Onion
    Packaged shrimp spice or pickling spices

1 Wash shrimps in colander under running cold water. (If frozen, they will separate easily and start to thaw.) Holding each shrimp rounded-shell-side down, break off feelers. Then run thumb under shell, bending shell back along side and easing shrimp out.
2 Remove the dark sand vein this way: Make a shallow cut down curve of back with a sharp-point knife, then lift out the black line, or sand vein, with tip of knife. To "butterfly" shrimps, cut the same curve deeper, then shrimps will spread open when they cook.
3 Drop shrimps into simmering water seasoned with sliced lemon, onion and packaged shrimp spice. (Or use pickling spices.) Simmer about 5 minutes for fresh shrimps, 10 minutes for frozen, or just until tender. Lift out at once with tongs or spoon.

Shrimp and Crab Cocktail
Makes 8 servings

1 pound medium-size fresh shrimps
    OR: 1 package (10 or 12 ounces) frozen shrimps in shells
1 teaspoon salt
1 small onion, sliced
2 slices lemon
1 bay leaf
1 can (about 5 ounces) king crabmeat
    PEPPY GUACAMOLE SAUCE (recipe follows)

1 Wash, shell and devein shrimps.
2 Half-fill a large frying pan with water; season with salt, onion, lemon and bay leaf; heat to boiling. Add shrimps; reheat until bubbling, then simmer 4 to 5 minutes, or just until tender, (do not overcook, as this toughens them); drain; chill.
3 Drain crabmeat and cut it into bite-size pieces, removing any thin bony tissue; chill.
4 Divide seafoods among 8 sherbet glasses, saving 8 shrimps for garnish; top with PEPPY GUACAMOLE SAUCE, then shrimps.
    PEPPY GUACAMOLE SAUCE—Halve, pit, peel and mash a medium-size ripe avocado in small bowl (you should have about 1 cup). Blend in ¼ cup mayonnaise, 2 tablespoons lemon juice, 1 teaspoon salt and ¼ teaspoon liquid red pepper seasoning. (If sauce is tightly covered, it will keep its rich green color for an hour before serving.) Makes 8 servings.

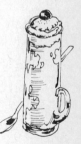

1765

Beach-Boy Shrimps
Makes 6 servings

1 pound fresh shrimps (or prawns) in shell
    OR: 2 packages (about 10 or 12 ounces each) frozen shrimps

6 tablespoons melted butter or margarine
2 tablespoons lemon juice
1 clove of garlic, minced
½ teaspoon salt
Pinch of cayenne

1 Peel shells from shrimps, thawing frozen ones just enough to handle; place on a 2-foot length of heavy-duty or double-thick aluminum foil; fold foil sides up, pinching ends together; roll ends in toward center to make 12-inch boat.
2 Combine remaining ingredients; pour over shrimps; triple-fold top of foil to make tight seal; take to beach. Or, if cooking at home, chill 1 to 2 hours.
3 To cook on grill: Open triple fold at top; fold foil sides back to make double thickness; squeeze ends for handles.
4 Grill over glowing coals, turning shrimps once or twice, 10 to 15 minutes, or until tender.
5 OR: To cook at home, place shrimps in large frying pan; sauté, stirring often, about 5 minutes.

Baked Stuffed Shrimps
Makes 3 servings

15 frozen deveined large shrimps
½ cup (1 stick) butter or margarine, melted
1 cup fine dry bread crumbs
¼ cup grated Parmesan cheese
½ teaspoon salt
½ teaspoon pepper
2 tablespoons lemon juice
2 tablespoons dry sherry

1 Place frozen shrimps in a baking pan, 8x8x2; brush each lightly with part of the melted butter or margarine. Heat in slow oven (325°) while preparing crumb topping.
2 Blend remaining butter or margarine with bread crumbs, cheese, salt, pepper, lemon juice and sherry in a small bowl; spoon evenly over shrimps.
3 Bake in slow oven (325°) 25 minutes, or until topping is golden.

South Seas Shrimp Kebabs
Meaty shrimps season in a zesty ginger-soy sauce, then broil to perfection.
Makes 6 servings

1½ pounds deveined shelled raw shrimps
1 can (1 pound) diet-pack pineapple chunks
2 tablespoons soy sauce

1 tablespoon cider vinegar
½ teaspoon ground ginger
2 tablespoons chopped parsley
3 cups hot cooked rice

1 Place shrimps in a shallow dish. Drain syrup from pineapple into a cup; stir in soy sauce, vinegar and ginger. Pour over shrimps; cover. Chill at least an hour to season.
2 Remove shrimps from marinade; thread each 3 shrimps and 3 pineapple chunks, alternately, onto 12 skewers; place on rack in broiler pan.
3 Broil, following range manufacturer's directions, 5 minutes; turn. Brush with marinade from dish. Broil 5 minutes longer, or just until shrimps are tender.
4 Combine chopped parsley and hot cooked rice; toss lightly to mix. Spoon onto serving plates; top with shrimp kebabs.

Shrimps Tempura
Makes 4 servings

2 pounds large fresh shrimps (or prawns) in shells
2 cups sifted flour
2 teaspoons salt
2 teaspoons sugar
1 teaspoon ground ginger
4 eggs
1 cup milk
Vegetable shortening or oil for frying

1 Shell shrimps carefully, leaving on tails; remove vein down back; dry shrimps on absorbent paper.
2 Combine flour, salt, sugar, ginger and eggs in medium-size bowl; beat until smooth; stir in milk (batter will be medium-thin).
3 Holding each shrimp by tail, dip in batter, then drop into 4-inch depth of hot fat heated to 380°.
4 Fry, turning once, about 3 minutes, or until golden-brown; drain on absorbent paper. Serve hot with: HOT-HOT MUSTARD, SPICY PLUM SAUCE or CHRYSANTHEMUM SOY SAUCE (recipe follows)

HOT-HOT MUSTARD—Combine ½ cup dry mustard, ¼ cup water and dash of turmeric in small bowl; stir until smooth. Makes about ¼ cup. This is a very hot mustard, so dip sparingly.

SPICY PLUM SAUCE—Combine 1 cup plum jam, 1 tablespoon cider vinegar, 1 teaspoon grated

Shrimps Tempura teamed with fancily-cut vegetables. ▶

onion, ½ teaspoon ground allspice, ¼ teaspoon ground ginger and a dash of cayenne in small saucepan; heat to boiling, stirring often; cool. Makes about 1 cup.

CHRYSANTHEMUM SOY SAUCE—Combine ½ cup water, ¼ cup soy sauce, 1 teaspoon sugar, ½ teaspoon prepared horseradish and ½ teaspoon ground ginger in small saucepan; bring to boiling; remove from heat at once and cool. Place 2 tablespoons grated fresh radishes in small bowl, slowly pour in sauce. Makes about ¾ cup.

Shrimp Sticks
Makes about 2 dozen

1 can (about 5 ounces) deveined shrimps
  Green pepper strips
1 can (5 ounces) water chestnuts
  Lemon juice
  HOT-HOT MUSTARD (recipe precedes)

1 Drain shrimps and rinse under cold running water; stick a tiny green pepper strip in middle of each and thread onto long thin wood or metal skewer; end with a water chestnut (if too large, cut in half).
2 Brush lightly with lemon juice; heat on a table grill or in your range broiler.
3 Serve hot with HOT-HOT MUSTARD.

Shrimps Imperial
Shrimps and vegetables go into the frying pan in separate mounds to cook the Far East way. Makes 4 servings

3 tablespoons peanut oil
1 Bermuda onion, sliced thin and separated into rings
2 cups thinly sliced celery
1 pound fresh shrimps, shelled and deveined
  OR: 1 package (12 ounces) frozen deveined shelled raw shrimps, thawed
½ pound Chinese snow peas
  OR: 1 package frozen Chinese pea pods, thawed
1 pound fresh spinach, washed and stemmed
1 can (5 ounces) water chestnuts, drained and sliced
⅓ cup soy sauce
1 tablespoon sugar
1 vegetable-bouillon cube
½ cup hot water
  Cooked hot rice

1768

1 Heat peanut oil in your largest frying pan (12-inch size is about right). Add onion rings and sliced celery in separate piles; sauté lightly just until they start to soften. Push each, keeping separate, to one side of pan.
2 Add shrimps, sauté, turning often, 5 minutes; push to one side. Place snow peas or pea pods, spinach and water chestnuts in separate mounds in same pan.
3 Mix soy sauce, sugar, bouillon cube and hot water in cup, stirring until cube dissolves. Pour in and around shrimps and vegetables, being careful not to cover water chestnuts so they will remain white; cover.
4 Heat to boiling; lower heat and simmer 10 minutes, or just until spinach wilts and shrimps are tender. Serve with hot rice.

Seafood Spaghetti Bowl
Shrimps, clams, and onions in garlic-seasoned butter make the sauce for favorite spaghetti. Makes 6 servings

1 pound thin spaghetti
½ cup (1 stick) butter or margarine
1 tablespoon bottled garlic spread
1½ pounds frozen, deveined, shelled, raw shrimps
¼ teaspoon pepper
1 can (about 7 ounces) minced clams
1 cup sliced green onions
2 tablespoons chopped parsley
  Grated Parmesan cheese

1 Cook spaghetti, following label directions; drain. Return to kettle; toss with half of the butter or margarine; keep hot.
2 While spaghetti cooks, melt remaining 4 tablespoons butter or margarine in large frying pan; stir in garlic spread and frozen shrimps. (No need to thaw.) Simmer, uncovered, stirring often, 10 minutes, or until shrimps are thawed.
3 Stir in pepper, clams and liquid, onions, and parsley; cover. Simmer 10 minutes longer, or until shrimps are tender.
4 When ready to serve, pile spaghetti into a large bowl; spoon sauce over. Serve with cheese to sprinkle over.

Confetti Noodle Squares with Shrimp Newburg Sauce
Dainty noodles, delicately seasoned with mild cheese, baked into a golden loaf, then cut into squares and served with a made-in-minutes shrimp sauce.

Shrimps and spaghetti? Prepared as Seafood Spaghetti Bowl they are a sensational scampi-pasta combination.

Bake at 350° for 35 to 40 minutes. Makes 6 servings

1 package (½ pound) fine noodles
2 tablespoons butter or margarine
2 eggs
1½ cups milk
1 tablespoon grated onion
1 teaspoon salt
1 teaspoon Worcestershire sauce
1½ cups grated mild Cheddar cheese (6 ounces)
½ cup soft bread crumbs (about 2 slices)
1 can (4 ounces) pimientos, finely chopped
3 tablespoons finely chopped parsley
   SHRIMP NEWBURG SAUCE (recipe follows)

1 Cook noodles in boiling salted water, following label directions; drain; return to kettle; stir in butter or margarine.
2 Beat eggs in small bowl; stir in milk, onion, salt and Worcestershire sauce; pour over noodles; add cheese, bread crumbs, pimientos and parsley; mix lightly; pour into well-buttered shallow baking dish, 10x6x2.
3 Bake in moderate oven (350°) 35 to 40 minutes, or until firm; cut into 6 squares to serve from baking dish, or remove squares with spatula to heated platter; serve with SHRIMP NEWBURG SAUCE.

Shrimp Newburg Sauce
Makes about 4 cups

2 cans (10 ounces each) frozen condensed cream of shrimp soup
1 can (6 ounces) sliced mushrooms
2 cans (about 5 ounces each) deveined shrimps, drained

1 Combine soup with mushrooms and liquid in top of double boiler; heat over boiling water, stirring occasionally, until soup is thawed.
2 Save 6 whole shrimps for garnish; dice remainder and add to soup mixture; heat thoroughly.

Shrimp Manicotti
Bake at 350° 30 minutes. Makes 8 servings

2 cans (10 ounces each) frozen cream of shrimp soup
1¼ cups milk

2 tablespoons dry sherry
1 can or jar (4 ounces) pimientos, drained and diced
2 bags (1 pound each) frozen shrimps, chopped
4 tablespoons (½ stick) butter or margarine
2 cups coarse soft bread crumbs (4 slices)
1 stalk celery, trimmed and chopped fine
1 tablespoon chopped parsley
½ teaspoon salt
1 package (½ pound) manicotti noodles (16 noodles)
1 cup shredded process American cheese (4 ounces)

1 Combine shrimp soup, milk, sherry and pimientos in a medium-size saucepan; heat, stirring constantly, until soup thaws and mixture is bubbly; remove from heat.
2 Sauté shrimps in butter or margarine in a large frying pan 2 minutes, or until tender; remove from heat. Stir in bread crumbs, celery, parsley and salt.
3 Cook manicotti noodles, 3 or 4 at a time, in a large amount of boiling salted water, following label directions; lift out carefully with a slotted spoon so as not to break them; drain.
4 Stuff shrimp mixture into noodles, using a teaspoon.
5 Pour about 1 cup of the soup-sauce into a 10-cup baking dish, to make a layer. Place part of the stuffed noodles in a row in sauce; repeat to make another layer of each, then pour any remaining sauce over top.
6 Bake, uncovered, in moderate oven (350°) 25 minutes. Sprinkle with cheese. Bake 5 minutes longer.

Newburg Noodles
Bake at 350° for 30 minutes. Makes 4 to 6 servings

1 package (½ pound) plain or twisted noodles or macaroni
1 can (10 ounces) frozen cream of shrimp soup
1 small can (⅔ cup) evaporated milk
½ cup mayonnaise or salad dressing
¼ cup grated sharp Cheddar cheese
¼ cup sherry, if desired
1 package (4 ounces) frozen French-fried onion rings

1 Cook noodles or macaroni following label directions; drain; place in 6-cup baking dish.
2 Heat frozen shrimp soup and evaporated milk in top of double boiler over boiling water, stir-

ring occasionally, until soup is thawed and sauce is smooth; stir in mayonnaise or salad dressing and cheese; heat until cheese is melted; stir in sherry, if desired; pour over noodles or macaroni; mix well.

3 Bake, covered, in moderate oven (350°) 20 minutes; uncover; arrange onion rings in single layer on top of noodles; continue baking 10 minutes longer, or until sauce is bubbly-hot and onion rings are crisp.

Shrimp and Corn Pudding
Bake at 325° about 50 minutes. Makes 4 servings

1 package (about 12 ounces) frozen deveined shrimps
3 eggs
1 cup milk
1 can (about 1 pound) cream-style corn
1 cup soft bread crumbs
1 medium-size onion, chopped
1 tablespoon sugar
1 teaspoon salt
⅛ teaspoon pepper
1 tablespoon melted butter or margarine
1 teaspoon Worcestershire sauce
1 tablespoon chopped parsley

1 Cook shrimps according to package directions; drain well; save a few whole ones; chop the rest.
2 Beat eggs slightly in large bowl; stir in remaining ingredients and chopped shrimps.
3 Turn into buttered 4-cup baking dish; place in baking pan; pour boiling water into pan to 1-inch depth.
4 Bake in slow oven (325°) about 50 minutes, or until knife inserted near center comes out clean; remove from water at once; garnish with whole shrimps.

Seashore Casserole
Bake at 350° for 30 minutes. Makes 6 servings

3 tablespoons butter or margarine
1 small onion, chopped (¼ cup)
2 tablespoons all-purpose flour
¼ teaspoon pepper
1 package (½ pound) shell macaroni, cooked and drained
2 cans (5 ounces each) shrimps, drained and cleaned
1½ cups buttermilk
1 cup (½ pound) cottage cheese

1 tablespoon melted butter or margarine
3 tablespoons fine dry bread crumbs

1 Melt butter or margarine in small frying pan; add onion and cook until tender and golden-brown; blend in flour and pepper; stir into cooked macaroni.
2 Add shrimps, buttermilk and cottage cheese; toss lightly; turn into buttered 6-cup baking dish.
3 Combine melted butter or margarine and bread crumbs; sprinkle over macaroni mixture.
4 Bake in moderate oven (350°) about 30 minutes, or until a rich golden brown on top.

Shrimps with Lemon Rice
Bake at 350° for 1¼ hours. Makes 8 servings

1 cup uncooked regular rice
2 teaspoons ground turmeric
1 teaspoon mustard seed
½ cup (1 stick) butter or margarine
2½ pounds raw shrimps, shelled and deveined
1 can or jar (7 ounces) pimientos, drained and diced
1 teaspoon salt
1 cup dry white wine
2 tablespoons lemon juice

1 Cook rice, following label directions.
2 Heat turmeric and mustard seed in butter or margarine in a large frying pan 2 to 3 minutes. Stir in shrimps; sauté 5 minutes; remove with a slotted spoon and place in a 10-cup refrigerator-to-oven baking dish.
3 Stir rice into drippings in pan; heat slowly, stirring constantly, until golden. Stir in pimientos and salt; spoon into baking dish.
4 Mix wine and lemon juice in a cup; stir into rice mixture. Cover; chill.
5 About 1 hour and 15 minutes before serving time, place baking dish, covered, in moderate oven (350°).
6 Bake 1 hour and 15 minutes, or until hot. Just before serving, fluff mixture with a fork.

1771

Party Paella
Bake at 375° for 1 hour and 15 minutes. Makes 8 to 10 servings

2 cans (5 ounces each) Vienna sausages
2 cans (about 5 ounces each) deveined shrimps
1 can (about 1 pound) peas
1 can (1 pint, 8 ounces) steamed clams in the shell

Party Paella is the kind of dish that draws "oohs and ahs." Believe it or not, it's easy to make.

1 cup frozen chopped onions (from a 12-ounce bag)
2 tablespoons olive oil
2 packages (6 ounces each) curried rice
2 cans (5 or 6 ounces each) boned chicken
1 pimiento, cut in thin strips

1 Drain liquids from sausages, shrimps and peas into a 4-cup measure; drain juice from clams into a small bowl. Wash clams under cold running water to remove any sand grains, then set aside with the other drained foods for Steps 4 and 6. Strain clam juice in bowl through cloth and add to liquids in measuring cup; add water, if needed, to make 4 cups. Set aside for Steps 3 and 5.
2 Sauté onions in olive oil just until soft in a large frying pan.
3 Remove the two flavor nuggets from packets of rice and add them to saved liquid in measuring cup. Stir rice and contents of the two seasoning packets into onion mixture in frying pan.
4 Layer half each of the rice mixture, chicken, sausages, shrimps and peas into a 12-cup baking dish; repeat to make another layer of each.
5 Pour the saved 4 cups liquid into same frying pan; add an additional ½ cup water and heat to boiling. Pour over layers in baking dish; cover dish.
6 Bake in moderate oven (375°) 1 hour; uncover. Place clams in shells on top; cover again.
7 Bake 15 minutes longer, or until rice is tender and clam shells open. Garnish with strips of pimiento.

Costa Brava Paella
Bake at 350° for 1 hour. Makes 6 servings

1 broiler-fryer (about 2 pounds), cut in serving size pieces
1 large onion, chopped (1 cup)
1 clove garlic, minced
1 cup uncooked regular rice
6 small slices salami (about 2 ounces), diced
2 teaspoons salt
1 teaspoon sugar
¼ teaspoon pepper
⅛ teaspoon crushed saffron
1 can (about 1 pound) tomatoes
1½ cups water
1 envelope instant chicken broth
   OR: 1 chicken bouillon cube
1 pound fresh shrimp, shelled and deveined
   OR: 1 package (12 ounces) frozen deveined shelled raw shrimps
1 can (4 ounces) pimientos, drained and cut in large pieces

1 Pull skin from chicken pieces, if you wish.

Place chicken, meaty side down, in a single layer on rack of broiler pan.
2 Broil, 4 inches from heat, 10 minutes; turn; broil 10 minutes longer, or until lightly browned; set aside for Step 4.
3 Pour drippings from broiler pan into a medium-size frying pan. Stir in onion and garlic; sauté until soft; spoon into a 12-cup baking dish with rice, salami, salt, sugar, pepper and saffron.
4 Combine tomatoes with water and instant chicken broth or bouillon cube in same frying pan; heat to boiling, crushing bouillon cube, if using, with a spoon. Stir into rice mixture with shrimps. Arrange chicken and pimientos on top; cover.
5 Bake in moderate oven (350°) 1 hour, or until liquid is absorbed and chicken is tender. Garnish with parsley and serve with chopped green onions to sprinkle on top, if you wish.

Sorrento Shrimp Scallop
Bake at 350° for 30 minutes. Makes enough for 2 meals, 6 servings each

1 cup uncooked regular rice
1 envelope instant vegetable broth
   OR: 1 envelope instant chicken broth
1¼ cups water
1 tablespoon cut chives
2 cans (10 ounces each) frozen cream of shrimp soup
1 cup milk
1 tablespoon Worcestershire sauce
1 teaspoon sherry
2 pounds frozen deveined shelled raw shrimps
2 packages (9 ounces each) frozen artichoke hearts
1 can (6 ounces) sliced mushrooms
2 slices white bread, cut into tiny cubes (1 cup)

1773

1 Cook rice in a large amount of boiling salted water in a kettle 20 minutes, or until almost tender. (It will finish cooking in the oven.) Drain; return to kettle.
2 Dissolve vegetable or chicken broth in the 1¼ cups water in a 2-cup measure; stir in chives; pour over drained rice.
3 While rice cooks, thaw frozen soup in top of a large double boiler over simmering water; blend in milk, Worcestershire sauce and sherry; remove from heat.
4 Cook shrimps and artichoke hearts, following label directions; drain. Set 6 of each aside for

garnish in Step 7. Fold remaining shrimps, artichokes and mushrooms and liquid into sauce.

5 Make alternate layers of shrimp mixture and rice, dividing evenly, and ending with shrimps, in two 8-cup shallow baking dishes. (One should be the freezer-to-oven kind.)

6 Cool one casserole, cover, label, date and freeze.

7 Arrange saved shrimps and artichoke hearts on top of second dish; sprinkle bread cubes around edge.

8 Bake in moderate oven (350°) 30 minutes, or until bubbly-hot.

Note: To bake frozen casserole, remove from freezer about two hours before serving time. Place, covered, in moderate oven (350°); bake 1 hour. Uncover; top with 1 cup bread cubes, if you wish. Bake 45 minutes longer, or until bubbly-hot.

Julie Eisenhower's Shrimp Curry

½ cup uncooked regular rice
1 package (8 ounces) frozen deveined shelled
  raw shrimps
2 tablespoons butter or margarine
2 tablespoons flour
½ teaspoon salt
  Dash each of pepper and paprika
1 cup milk
3 tablespoons catsup
½ to 1 teaspoon curry powder

1 Cook rice, following label directions.

2 Cook shrimp, following label directions.

3 Make sauce; Melt butter or margarine in medium-size saucepan; stir in flour, salt and pepper; cook, stirring constantly, just until bubbly. Stir in milk; continue cooking and stirring until sauce thickens and boils 1 minute. Stir in catsup, curry powder and paprika, blending well.

4 Add shrimp to sauce; keep over low heat until heated through.

5 Serve shrimp in sauce over rice.

Speedy Shrimp Wiggle in Patty Shells
Makes 6 servings

1 package (10 ounces) frozen patty shells
1 can (10 ounces) frozen cream of shrimp soup
1 cup light cream or table cream
1 bag (1½ pounds) frozen deveined shelled raw
  shrimps

An elegantly Italianesque shrimp dish: Sorrento Shrimp Scallop, combining frozen shrimps and artichoke hearts with rice and cream of shrimp soup.

1 slice lemon
1 bay leaf
1 package (10 ounces) frozen peas in cream
  sauce

1 Bake patty shells, following label directions; keep hot.

2 Place frozen soup in the top of a large double boiler; heat, stirring often, over simmering water until thawed; stir in cream.

3 While soup thaws, place frozen shrimps in a 1-inch depth of simmering water seasoned with lemon slice and bay leaf in a large frying pan; simmer 10 minutes, or just until tender. Lift out with a slotted spoon and drain, then stir into soup mixture.

4 Cook frozen peas, following label directions; stir into soup mixture. Heat until hot.

5 Place patty shells on serving plates; spoon shrimp sauce, dividing evenly, into shells.

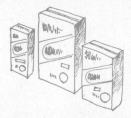

Savory Shrimps and Chicken Marengo
For a festive flair, serve this saucy combination in scallop shells.
Makes 8 servings

1 chicken breast (about 12 ounces)
4 tablespoons vegetable oil
½ teaspoon monosodium glutamate
1 large onion, chopped (1 cup)
1 clove garlic, minced
2 tablespoons all-purpose flour
1 can (2¼ ounces) deviled ham
1 can (8 ounces) stewed tomatoes
1 can (3 or 4 ounces) whole mushrooms
1 teaspoon Worcestershire sauce
1 pound fresh shrimps, shelled and deveined
  Chopped parsley

1 Pull skin from chicken breast; cut meat from bones in two large pieces, then cut into 1-inch pieces.

2 Brown in 2 tablespoons of the vegetable oil in a medium-size frying pan; sprinkle with monosodium glutamate; cover. Cook slowly 15 minutes, or until tender.

3 While chicken cooks, sauté onion and garlic until soft in remaining 2 tablespoons vegetable oil in a second medium-size frying pan; blend in flour; cook, stirring constantly, until bubbly.

4 Blend in deviled ham, then stir in tomatoes, mushrooms and liquid and Worcestershire

1775

sauce. Cook, stirring constantly, until mixture thickens and boils 1 minute; remove chicken from frying pan with a slotted spoon and stir into sauce.

5 Stir shrimps into chicken drippings in frying pan; cook slowly, turning once, 10 minutes, or until tender. Stir into sauce mixture.

6 Spoon into a chafing-dish, keep-hot server or scallop shells; sprinkle with chopped parsley. Serve with small triangles of crisp toast, if you wish.

Gulf Coast Gumbo
Makes 4 servings

1 small bunch green onions, chopped
1 medium-size green pepper, chopped
1 small hot red pepper, chopped (about 1 tablespoon)
1 clove of garlic, sliced
3 tablespoons melted butter or margarine
2 cups sliced okra (½ pound)
1 can (about 1 pound) tomatoes
2 cans (about 13 ounces each) chicken broth
1 bay leaf
¼ teaspoon salt
1 package (12 ounces) frozen oysters, thawed
1 package (5 ounces) frozen shelled deveined shrimps, thawed
1 package (6 ounces) frozen crabmeat, thawed and cut into ½-inch pieces
1 teaspoon filé powder*
3 cups hot cooked rice

1 Sauté green onions, green and red peppers and garlic in melted butter or margarine in large saucepan 5 minutes, or just until tender.

2 Add okra, tomatoes, chicken broth, bay leaf and salt; bring to boiling; reduce heat; simmer 1 hour.

3 Add oysters, shrimps, crabmeat and filé powder: simmer 5 minutes.

4 Place a mound of rice in each soup bowl or plate; spoon hot gumbo mixture over.

* Filé powder thickens and flavors gumbo, but may be omitted if you wish.

Aloha Rice-Bowl Salad with Marinated Shrimps
Plan this spectacular salad for your next summer party. It's a hostess' joy, for everything in it is a make-ahead.
Makes 6 servings

1 cup uncooked regular rice

1 tablespoon vegetable oil or olive oil
1 teaspoon cider vinegar
1 teaspoon soy sauce
1 can (14 ounces) frozen pineapple chunks, thawed
1 cup celery, sliced diagonally
¼ cup chopped green onions
½ cup mayonnaise
MARINATED SHRIMPS (recipe follows)
Lettuce

1 Cook rice, following label directions; if needed, drain, and place colander over hot water for 2 to 3 minutes to dry and fluff up rice kernels.

2 Mix vegetable oil or olive oil, vinegar and soy sauce in 6-cup bowl (salad will be molded in it); stir in rice and toss lightly.

3 Drain thawed pineapple chunks (save syrup for next step); stir pineapple, celery and green onions into rice mixture.

4 Blend mayonnaise with 2 tablespoons pineapple syrup from Step 3; stir into rice mixture; pat down lightly; chill at least 30 minutes.

5 Unmold onto serving platter; top with 3 MARINATED SHRIMPS; serve remaining shrimps with lettuce.

Marinated Shrimps
They're delicately sweet and tender when cooked quickly in gently bubbling seasoned water.
Makes 6 servings

1½ pounds large raw shrimps in shells (16 to 24 to each pound)
4 cups water
1 small onion, sliced
2 lemon slices
Handful of celery tops
1 sprig parsley
1 teaspoon salt
6 peppercorns
2 whole cloves
1 bay leaf
2 tablespoons vegetable oil
2 tablespoons lemon juice

1 Wash shrimps in colander under running cold water; shell by splitting feelers open and turning shell back, then easing shrimp out with force of water; make a shallow cut down back of each; remove black line, or sand vein, with tip of knife; make cut a bit deeper so shrimps will curl up when cooked.

2 Heat water, onion, lemon, celery tops, parsley, salt, peppercorns, cloves and bay leaf to boiling in large frying pan, then simmer 2 to 3 minutes.

The original Marengo, invented by Napoleon's chef, contained chicken. Savory Shrimps and Chicken Marengo one-ups original.

3 Drop in prepared shrimps; heat just to boiling, then simmer 3 to 5 minutes, or until shrimps are pink (do not let water boil; it will overcook and toughen them).
4 Remove with slotted spoon to a medium-size bowl; sprinkle with mixture of vegetable oil and lemon juice; cover; chill until serving time.

Seaside Macaroni Salad
Makes 6 servings

½ cup uncooked elbow macaroni
1 package (1 pound) frozen deveined shelled shrimps
½ cup bottled French dressing
1 package (10 ounces) frozen baby lima beans, cooked, drained and chilled
½ cup finely chopped celery
½ cup mayonnaise or salad dressing
2 tablespoons finely chopped parsley
Boston lettuce
2 small tomatoes, cut in very thin wedges

1 Cook macaroni, following label directions; drain; place in a large bowl.
2 Cook shrimp, following label directions; drain; add to macaroni. Drizzle French dressing over top; toss lightly to mix. Chill at least an hour to season.
3 Just before serving, add limas and celery to macaroni mixture; fold in mayonnaise or salad dressing. Spoon into a lettuce-lined bowl; place tomato wedges around edge in bowl.

Shrimp and Lobster Salad in Artichoke Petal Cups
Makes 4 servings

4 small fresh artichokes
Boiling salted water
Olive oil
1 can (about 6 ounces) flaked lobster, drained
1 can (about 5 ounces) deveined shrimps, drained
½ cup diced celery

1777

¼ cup dairy sour cream
1 tablespoon chili sauce
1 tablespoon lemon juice
  Lemon wedges

1 Snip tops and prickly leaf tips and remove stem bottoms from artichokes; cook, covered, in boiling salted water seasoned with a few drops olive oil 30 to 45 minutes or until tender. Drain; let stand until cool enough to handle; separate leaves enough to cut out "choke" at base; chill.
2 Mix together all remaining ingredients except lemon wedges and chill well.
3 To serve, spoon shrimp and lobster mixture into artichoke petal cups and garnish with lemon wedges.

●

Bayou Shrimp Salad
Makes 8 to 10 servings

1 cup uncooked regular rice
1 teaspoon sugar
½ teaspoon grated lime peel
2 tablespoons lime juice
1½ cups diced cooked ham (½ pound)
1 cup sliced celery
½ cup diced green pepper
1 package (12 ounces) frozen deveined shelled raw shrimps
1 package (10 ounces) frozen whole okra
6 tablespoons bottled thin French dressing
½ cup mayonnaise or salad dressing
1 tablespoon chopped parsley
1 cup halved cherry tomatoes
  Salt and pepper
  Romaine

1 Cook rice, following label directions; drain well. Place in a large bowl; stir in sugar, lime peel and juice, ham, celery and green pepper.
2 Cook shrimps and okra in separate medium-size saucepans, following label directions; drain well.
3 Dice remaining shrimps, but leave okra whole; add shrimps and okra to rice-ham mixture; drizzle French dressing over; toss to mix. Chill at least 30 minutes to season and blend flavors.
4 Just before serving, fold in mayonnaise or salad dressing, parsley and cherry tomatoes. Season to taste with salt and pepper.

Shrimp and Lobster Salad in Artichoke Petal Cups—an excellent choice for a small ladies' luncheon.

5 Spoon into a deep bowl lined with romaine; garnish with the saved shrimps and okra and a single whole cherry tomato, if you wish.

Shimmering Shrimp Aspic
Makes 6 servings

3 cans (about 14 ounces each) chicken broth
3 envelopes unflavored gelatin
2 packages (1 pound each) frozen deveined shelled shrimp
  Watercress
  Pitted ripe olives, slivered
1 cup mayonnaise or salad dressing
2 tablespoons lemon juice
1 teaspoon grated onion
3 hard-cooked eggs, shelled and coarsely chopped
½ cup diced celery

1 Skim fat from chicken broth.
2 Soften gelatin in chicken broth about 5 minutes in a large saucepan. Heat, stirring constantly, until gelatin dissolves. Pour into a medium-size bowl; cool.
3 Cook shrimp, following label directions; drain; cool. Set aside 6 shrimp for decoration; cut remainder into bite-size pieces; place in a large bowl; cover; chill.
4 Pour ½ cup of the cooled gelatin mixture into an 8x8x2 pan; chill. (Use for platter decoration in Step 10.)
5 Pour ½ cup of the remaining gelatin mixture into a 9x5x3 loaf pan. Chill until sticky-firm.
6 Arrange reserved whole shrimp, with watercress sprigs and olives on the aspic in loaf pan to make a pretty design. Spoon ½ cup of the remaining gelatin mixture carefully over the design, a little at a time, chilling briefly after each addition. Then chill completed design layer till it is sticky-firm.
7 Stir mayonnaise or salad dressing and lemon juice into remaining gelatin mixture. Place bowl in a pan of ice and water to speed setting. Chill, stirring several times, until as thick as unbeaten egg white.
8 Fold in onion, chopped eggs, shrimp and celery. Pour carefully over sticky-firm aspic layer in loaf pan. Chill until firm, about 4 hours. (Overnight is best.)
9 Just before serving, loosen salad around edges with a knife; dip pan *very quickly* in and out of hot water. Cover pan with serving plate; turn upside down; gently lift off pan.
10 Cut small triangles from firm aspic in square pan. Arrange as decorative border around salad. Chill until serving time.
11 To serve, cut salad into 6 slices; garnish each serving with some of the aspic triangles.

Basic Boiled Lobster
Makes 4 servings

4 small live lobsters (about 1 pound each)
  Boiling salted water
½ cup melted butter

1 Drop live lobsters into a very large kettle of boiling salted water; cover. Keep heat high and cook 10 to 15 minutes. Lobsters will turn bright red. Remove at once with tongs and drain.
2 With a sharp knife, split lobsters down the center (underside) and brush liberally with melted butter. Or, if you prefer, simply place 1 lobster and a small ramekin of melted butter on each of 4 plates. Put out the lobster crackers and picks for getting every last bit of meat. Each person then, can crack open his own lobster, twist out the meat and dunk into melted butter.

Capetown Lobster
Makes 6 servings

12 frozen South African lobster tails (4 packages, 10 ounces each)
1 lemon, sliced
1 tablespoon mixed whole spices
  CURRY DIP (recipe follows)

1 Cook lobster tails in boiling salted water with lemon and mixed whole spices, following label directions; drain.
2 When shells are cool enough to handle, cut with scissors through thick membrane on each side where it joins to hard shell; remove; peel hard shells back with one hand, pulling lobster meat out with the other.
3 Place in a colander over boiling water; cover lightly and steam to keep hot. (Or prepare early in day, chill lobster, then reheat at serving time.) Serve with CURRY DIP.

1779

Curry Dip
A thick spicy sauce—so right with mild-flavor lobster tails.
Makes 1½ cups

1 large onion, chopped (1 cup)
1 cup water
1 tablespoon curry powder
1 chicken-bouillon cube
¼ teaspoon salt

¼ teaspoon ground ginger
1 cup applesauce
4 teaspoons sugar
2 teaspoons lemon juice

1 Cook onion slowly in ½ cup water in small saucepan, stirring often, 10 minutes, or until onion is soft.
2 Stir in curry powder; cook 1 minute; add bouillon cube, salt, ginger, applesauce, sugar and remaining ½ cup water; mix well.
3 Simmer, stirring often, 5 minutes, or until thick. Just before serving, stir in lemon juice.

●

Skewered Lobster
Makes 4 servings

4 small frozen lobster tails, about 8 ounces each
½ cup vegetable oil
2 tablespoons soy sauce
1 tablespoon minced onion
1 teaspoon salt
1 teaspoon dry mustard
1 teaspoon ground ginger
1 clove of garlic, minced
1 teaspoon pepper
HOT DIP (recipe follows)

1 Cook lobster tails in boiling water, following label directions; drain, let cool, then with scissors cut away meat from shell.
2 Combine remaining ingredients; pour over lobster tails in shallow dish; cover; let stand in refrigerator 3 to 4 hours, basting often with marinade.
3 Thread lobster tails on individual skewers; grill over glowing coals, turning and basting often with marinade, about 10 minutes, or until heated through.
4 Serve with HOT DIP.

HOT DIP—Combine 1 cup catsup, 3 tablespoons prepared mustard, 1 tablespoon prepared horseradish, 1 teaspoon Worcestershire sauce, ½ teaspoon garlic powder and ¼ teaspoon freshly grated or cracked pepper in small bowl; chill to blend flavors. Makes 1¼ cups.

1780

Lobster Adventure
Makes 6 servings

3 small frozen South African lobster tails, thawed
1 package (10 ounces) frozen unbreaded scallops, thawed

1 can (about 7 ounces) crabmeat, drained
3 tablespoons butter or margarine
1 can (10 ounces) frozen cream of shrimp soup
Dash of white pepper
2 tablespoons dry sherry

1 Remove lobster meat from shells; cut lobster, scallops and crabmeat into bite-size pieces.
2 Sauté seafoods, stirring constantly, in butter or margarine in a large frying pan 5 minutes. Add shrimp soup and heat, stirring constantly, until bubbly. Stir in pepper and sherry.
3 Serve over cooked rice.

Baked Lobster Newburg
Chunks of lobster meat bake in a creamy sauce in their natural shells and en coquille for another company fancy.
Bake at 450° for 7 minutes. Makes 6 servings

4 packages (10 ounces each) South African lobster tails
2 cans (10 ounces each) frozen cream of shrimp soup
½ cup light cream or table cream
½ cup chopped sweet red pepper
2 teaspoons lemon juice
¼ teaspoon curry powder
1 tablespoon dry sherry
2 tablespoons chopped watercress
½ cup buttered soft bread crumbs (1 slice)
1 lemon, cut in 6 wedges
Watercress

1 Cook lobster tails in boiling salted water, following label directions; drain; cool.
2 With scissors, cut through the thick membrane on underside of shell and remove. Take out lobster meat by peeling hard shell back with fingers of one hand and pulling meat toward you with the other. Place 6 shells in a large shallow pan for Step 5 and discard remaining.
3 Cut lobster meat into about ½-inch-thick slices; place in a medium-size bowl.
4 Heat shrimp soup slowly until thawed in a small saucepan; stir in cream, red pepper, lemon juice, curry powder and sherry; continue heating until bubbly. Stir in chopped watercress; pour over lobster meat; toss lightly to mix.
5 Spoon about ⅓ cup into each lobster shell, using a slotted spoon so excess sauce will drip back into bowl; sprinkle with bread crumbs. Chill remaining lobster mixture for LOBSTER EN COQUILLE *(recipe follows)*.
6 Bake shells in very hot oven (450°) 7 minutes, or until bubbly and crumbs are toasty-golden.

Two seafood classics, one made from the other: Baked Lobster Newburg and descended from it, delectable Lobster en Coquille to be frozen and enjoyed later.

7 Place on a serving platter; garnish with a bouquet of lemon wedges and watercress.

•

Lobster en Coquille

Your freezer dividend: Individual casseroles of creamy lobster and rice with a soufflélike cap. Bake at 400° for 1 hour and 25 minutes. Makes 6 servings

1 package (10 ounces) frozen cut asparagus
3 cups lobster meat and sauce (from BAKED LOBSTER NEWBURG)
3 cups cooked rice
3 tablespoons butter or margarine
¼ cup sifted all-purpose flour
¼ teaspoon salt
½ cup milk
2 eggs, separated

1 Cook asparagus, following label directions; drain; cool. Combine with lobster mixture in a medium-size bowl.
2 Spoon rice into 6 scrubbed seashells or individual shallow baking dishes. Spoon lobster mixture, dividing evenly, on top. Place shells in a shallow pan for easy handling. Wrap in foil, label, date and freeze.
3 About 1½ hours before serving, remove pan from freezer. (Do not uncover.)
4 Bake in hot oven (400°) 1 hour.
5 While shells bake, melt butter or margarine in a small saucepan; blend in flour and salt; stir in milk. Cook, stirring constantly, until mixture forms a thick smooth ball that follows spoon around pan; remove from heat at once. Let stand to cool slightly.
6 Beat egg whites until they form soft peaks in a medium-size bowl.
7 Beat egg yolks, one at a time, into slightly cooled mixture; fold into beaten egg whites until no streaks of white remain.
8 Remove partly baked shells from oven; uncover. Spoon about ¼ cup of topping mixture on each.
9 Bake 25 minutes longer, or until topping is puffy-golden. Serve at once.
Note: If baking casseroles without freezing, bake in hot oven (400°) 25 minutes, or until topping is puffy-golden.

1781

THE SEA'S BOUNTY

Mardi Gras Seafood Bake

A colorful holiday treat. Lobster, clams and fish fillets team with rice in a seasoned tomato sauce.

Bake at 350° for 1 hour. Makes 6 servings

    1 large onion, chopped (1 cup)
    1 clove garlic, minced
    ¼ cup olive oil or vegetable oil
    1½ cups uncooked regular rice
    6 strands saffron, crushed
    1 envelope instant vegetable broth
      OR: 1 vegetable-bouillon cube
    1½ teaspoons salt
    1 can (1 pound) tomatoes
    1 bottle (8 ounces) clam juice
    1 cup water
    1 package (1 pound) frozen haddock or
      flounder fillets, thawed
    1 can (11 ounces) minced clams
    1 package (10 ounces) frozen South African
      lobster tails
    3 tablespoons butter or margarine, melted
    1 package (10 ounces) frozen peas

1 Sauté onion and garlic in olive oil or vegetable oil until soft in a large frying pan; remove from pan.

2 Stir rice and saffron into drippings in pan; sauté, stirring constantly, until rice is golden; return onion mixture, then stir in vegetable broth or bouillon cube, salt, tomatoes, clam juice and water. Heat to boiling; remove from heat.

3 Set aside 3 of the fish fillets for Step 5, then cut remaining into bite-size pieces; stir into rice mixture with clams and liquid. Spoon into a deep 12-cup baking dish; cover.

4 Bake in moderate oven (350°) 30 minutes.

5 While casserole bakes, cook lobster tails in boiling salted water, following label directions; drain; cool until easy to handle. With scissors cut through the thick membrane on underside of shell and remove. Take out lobster meat by peeling hard shell back with fingers of one hand and pulling meat toward you with the other; split each piece of meat in half. Roll up saved fish fillets.

6 Arrange lobster meat and rolled fillets on top of rice mixture in baking dish; brush with part of the melted butter or margarine; cover.

7 Bake 30 minutes longer, or until rice and fish are tender.

1782

Summer seafood salads (clockwise from upper left): Crab and Fruit Bowl, Cape Cod Scallops Salad, Lobster Salad Supreme and Glazed Tuna-Salmon Mold.

Worthy of the finest sterling dish—Mardi Gras Seafood Bake made with canned and frozen foods.

8 Cook peas, following label directions; season with remaining melted butter or margarine; spoon around edge of dish. Garnish fish rolls with pimiento, if you wish.

●

Lobster-Rice Soufflé

It puffs high and handsome—and stays there—without any sleight-of-hand.

Bake at 325° for 1 hour. Makes 6 servings

¼ uncooked regular rice
¼ teaspoon salt (for rice)
¾ cup boiling water
4 eggs
4 tablespoons (½ stick) butter or margarine
4 tablespoons all-purpose flour
½ teaspoon salt (for sauce)
1 cup milk
1 can (6 ounces) lobster meat, drained, boned and cut into bite-size pieces
SWISS-CHEESE SAUCE (recipe follows)

1 Stir rice and ¼ teaspoon salt into boiling water in small saucepan; cover; simmer 20 minutes, or until rice is tender and water is absorbed.

2 Separate eggs, putting whites into medium-size bowl, yolks into large bowl.
3 Melt butter or margarine over low heat in medium-size saucepan. Stir in flour and ½ teaspoon salt; cook, stirring all the time, just until mixture bubbles. Stir in milk slowly; continue cooking and stirring until sauce is very thick and boils 1 minute; remove from heat.
4 Beat egg whites just until they form soft peaks.
5 Beat egg yolks well; slowly stir in cream sauce, cooked rice and lobster. Lightly fold in beaten egg whites until no streaks of sauce or egg white remain. Pour into ungreased 8-cup deep baking dish.
6 Set dish in baking pan on oven shelf; pour in boiling water to depth of 1 inch.
7 Bake in slow oven (325°) 1 hour, or until top is firm and puffy-golden. Serve at once with SWISS-CHEESE SAUCE.

SWISS-CHEESE SAUCE—Melt 2 tablespoons butter or margarine over low heat in medium-size saucepan. Stir in 2 tablespoons all-purpose flour, ½ teaspoon salt and ½ teaspoon dry mustard, then cook, stirring all the time, just until mixture bubbles. Stir in 1½ cups milk slowly; continue cooking and stirring until sauce thickens and boils 1 minute. Stir in 1 cup (4 ounces) freshly grated process Swiss cheese until melted. Makes 2 cups.

Seafare Grill
Makes 6 servings

18 large unshelled fresh or frozen shrimps (about 1 pound)
⅓ cup lemon juice
2 tablespoons vegetable oil
1 small clove of garlic, crushed
¼ teaspoon salt
¼ teaspoon dry mustard
6 frozen South African lobster tails (3 packages, 10 ounces each)
½ cup (1 stick) butter or margarine
2 teaspoons curry powder
3 medium-size bananas

1 Wash shrimps; drain; loosen shells but leave on; place in medium-size bowl; combine lemon juice, vegetable oil, garlic, salt and mustard, and pour over shrimps; let stand at least 30 minutes to marinate, then thread onto skewers.
2 Cut around thin undershell membrane of frozen lobster tails (no need to thaw them) and remove it; crack shells by bending tail back; score meat lengthwise with ½-inch-deep cut.
3 Melt butter or margarine with curry powder in small saucepan; brush on lobster tails.
4 Grill over hot coals, shell side down, brushing often with curry-butter; turn with meat side down, and grill, brushing with curry-butter, until lobster is tender. Time depends on heat of fire and distance from coals. Do not overcook lobster tails. A good guide is 10 to 15 minutes for total time.
5 Grill shrimps on skewers alongside lobster on grill, basting often with their marinade, 5 to 10 minutes, or until they turn pink. (Do not overcook shrimps either.)
6 Cut unpeeled bananas in half lengthwise; brush with curry-butter; place, skin side down, on grill, grill 5 minutes.
7 Serve with cut lemon or lime wedges and more melted curry-butter mixture, if you wish.

Lobster Salad Supreme
Pile salad into lobster shells and garnish with the jumbo claws.
Makes 4 servings

4 small live lobsters (about 1 pound each)
1 cup chopped celery

1 cup chopped green pepper
½ cup mayonnaise or salad dressing
1 tablespoon lime juice
Salt and pepper
TOMALLEY-STUFFED EGGS (recipe follows)

1 Drop live lobsters into a very large kettle of rapidly boiling salted water; cover. Keep heat high and cook 10 to 15 minutes. Lobsters will turn a bright red. Remove at once with tongs; drain until cool enough to handle. (If you do not have a very large kettle, cook lobsters, 2, or even 1, at a time, adding more water and heating to boiling each time.)
2 Remove meat from each lobster, saving shell for restuffing, this way: Place lobster on its back; twist off the 2 large claws and set aside for Step 4. Cut lobster down middle from head to tail, being careful not to cut through hard shell of back. Twist and gently pull small claws away. Cut away the thin membrane on either side of tail with kitchen scissors and lift out meat. Save the green tomalley (liver), and pink coral (roe), if any, for stuffing eggs.
3 Discard the stomach sac or "lady" in back of head, black vein running from head to tail and spongy gray tissue.
4 Set the 4 lobster shells and 8 large ends of claws from Step 2 aside. Crack rest of claw pieces; remove meat with a metal pick and place in a medium-size bowl. Dice meat from tail and add to bowl.
5 Stir in celery, green pepper, mayonnaise or salad dressing, lime juice and salt and pepper to taste. Pile back into lobster shells, dividing evenly.
6 Place on salad plates; garnish each with the 2 large claw pieces, cracked, and watercress, if you wish. Serve with TOMALLEY-STUFFED EGGS.

TOMALLEY-STUFFED EGGS—Shell 4 hard-cooked eggs and halve crosswise. Remove yolks and press through a sieve into a small bowl. Blend in saved lobster tomalley and roe and ¼ cup mayonnaise or salad dressing; pile back into whites. Garnish each with a tiny square of green pepper. Makes 4 servings.

1785

Cucumber-Rice Ring with Stuffed Lobster
Pair this cucumber-topped rice salad with stuffed lobster for a party meal.
Makes 8 servings

Cucumber Layer
1 envelope unflavored gelatin
2 tablespoons sugar
1 teaspoon salt
1½ cups boiling water

¼ cup lemon juice
½ cucumber, sliced thin

Rice-Salad Layer
8 cups cooked rice (2 cups uncooked)
2 cups chopped celery
6 hard-cooked eggs, chopped
½ cup chopped green pepper
½ cup chopped pimientos
½ cup chopped parsley
¼ cup chopped stuffed green olives
1 envelope unflavored gelatin
2 teaspoons salt
½ cup water
½ cup cream for whipping
2 cups mayonnaise
  STUFFED LOBSTER (recipe follows)
  Lettuce
  Lemon slices

1 Make cucumber layer: Mix gelatin, sugar and salt in 2-cup measure; stir in boiling water until gelatin is dissolved; stir in lemon juice. Chill until syrupy-thick.
2 Place a 12-cup mold in a larger bowl of ice and water; pour ½ cup syrupy gelatin into mold; arrange a ring of cucumber slices, overlapping, on top. Let layer set until sticky-firm, then carefully spoon remaining syrupy gelatin over; chill until sticky-firm.
3 Make rice-salad layer: Combine rice, celery, eggs, green pepper, pimientos, parsley and olives in large bowl.
4 Soften gelatin with salt in water in a 1-cup measure; heat over hot water until dissolved; cool.
5 Beat cream until stiff in medium-size bowl; fold in mayonnaise; stir in cooled gelatin mixture until well blended; fold into rice mixture. Spoon over sticky-firm cucumber layer in mold; chill 12 hours or overnight, or until firm.
6 To unmold, run a sharp-tip thin-blade knife around top of mold, then dip mold *very quickly* in and out of a pan of hot water. Or, after loosening around top, tip mold from side to side, shaking gently to loosen gelatin from side enough to break vacuum at bottom. Cover mold with serving platter; turn upside down, then gently lift off mold.
7 Arrange STUFFED LOBSTER on lettuce around mold; tuck in lemon slices.

Stuffed Lobster
French-dressing marinade gives this lobster its tart spicy flavor.
Makes 8 servings

8 frozen South African lobster tails (3 or 4 packages, 10 ounces each)
1 lemon, sliced
1 tablespoon mixed whole spices
⅔ cup bottled thin French dressing

1 Cook lobster tails in boiling salted water with lemon and mixed whole spices, following label directions; drain.
2 When shells are cool enough to handle, cut with scissors through thick membrane on each side where it joins hard shell; remove membrane. Take out lobster meat by peeling hard shell back with one hand and pulling meat out with the other. Chill shells for Step 4.
3 Cut lobster meat into bite-size pieces; place in a large bowl; pour French dressing over, tossing lobster lightly until coated. Cover; chill several hours.
4 Spoon marinated lobster into shells, dividing evenly.

●

Cannes Clam Puff
Clam fans will like the delicate flavor of this beauty. Over all goes a creamy topper sparked with bits of leeks.
Bake at 350° for 50 minutes. Makes 4 servings

1 can (about 8 ounces) minced clams
  Skim milk
¼ cup instant-type flour
1 teaspoon salt
¼ teaspoon liquid red pepper seasoning
4 eggs, separated
  LEEK SAUCE (recipe follows)

1 Grease well a 4-cup soufflé dish or a straight-side baking dish.
2 Drain liquid from clams into a 1-cup measure; add skim milk to make 1 cup. Set clams aside for Step 4. Combine liquid with flour, salt and red pepper seasoning in a small saucepan; cook, stirring constantly, until mixture thickens and boils 1 minute; remove from heat. Let cool while beating eggs.
3 Beat egg whites just until they form soft peaks in a medium-size bowl.
4 Beat egg yolks well in a large bowl; beat in cooled sauce very slowly; stir in minced clams, then fold in beaten egg whites until no streaks of white or yellow remain. Pour into prepared dish.
5 Set dish in a baking pan; place on oven shelf; pour boiling water into pan to a depth of about 1 inch.
6 Bake in moderate oven (350°) 50 minutes, or until puffy-firm and golden. Remove from pan of water. Serve at once with LEEK SAUCE.

  LEEK SAUCE—Trim 1 medium-size leek, then

1786

slice thin. (It should measure about 1 cup.) If leeks are not available in your area, use 1 medium-size onion, peeled and coarsely chopped. Parboil leek or onion in water to cover in a small saucepan 5 minutes; drain well. Combine 1 cup skim milk, 2 tablespoons butter or margarine, 2 tablespoons instant-type flour and ¼ teaspoon salt in a small saucepan. Cook, stirring constantly, until sauce thickens and boils 1 minute. Stir in drained leek or onion. Makes about 1½ cups.

●

New England Oyster Scallop
Succulent oysters bake plump and moist between layers of rich parsley-butter crumbs.
Bake at 350° for 30 minutes. Makes 4 to 6 servings

4 tablespoons (½ stick) butter or margarine
2 cups coarse soda-cracker crumbs (about 24)
½ cup chopped parsley
1 teaspoon salt
¼ teaspoon pepper
1 pint (about 24) oysters
   OR: 2 cans (7 ounces each) frozen oysters, thawed
½ cup light cream or table cream
1 teaspoon Worcestershire sauce

1 Melt butter or margarine in saucepan; remove from heat; stir in cracker crumbs, parsley, salt and pepper.
2 Drain and save juice from oysters. Sprinkle ⅓ of crumb mixture into a 9-inch pie plate; layer half the oysters on top, then half of remaining crumbs and rest of oysters.

Stuffed Lobster is a snappy seafood salad made of frozen lobster tails and a bottled French dressing.

3 Combine saved oyster juice, cream and Worcestershire sauce in 2-cup measure; pour over top; sprinkle with remaining crumbs.
4 Bake in moderate oven (350°) 30 minutes, or until top is golden. Serve hot, plain or with chili sauce.

Ribbon Oyster Scallop

Bake at 425° for 10 minutes. Makes 8 servings

2 cans (10 ounces each) frozen condensed oyster stew
2 cans (about 7 ounces each) oysters
1 can (3 or 4 ounces) sliced mushrooms
2 cups crushed oyster crackers
Few drops liquid red pepper seasoning
2 tablespoons chopped parsley
2 tablespoons butter or margarine

1 Heat oyster stew very slowly until thawed in a large heavy saucepan; lift out oysters with a slotted spoon and set aside in a cup for Step 4.
2 Drain liquids from canned oysters and mushrooms into stew in saucepan; heat just to boiling.
3 Stir in 1½ cups of the crushed crackers; heat, stirring constantly, 3 minutes, or until mixture thickens; remove from heat.
4 Stir in liquid red pepper seasoning, oysters and mushrooms. Spoon into a 6-cup shallow baking dish; sprinkle with chopped parsley.
5 Melt butter or margarine in a small saucepan; add remaining ½ cup crushed crackers; mix well; spoon in rows over oyster mixture.
6 Bake in hot oven (425°) 10 minutes, or until crumbs are golden.

Golden Gate Oyster Boats

Crusty-golden oysters spill out of buttery rolls in this hot sandwich.
Makes 6 servings

1 pint (about 24) oysters
OR: 2 cans (7 ounces each) frozen oysters, thawed
1 egg
½ teaspoon salt
¼ teaspoon pepper
½ cup cracker crumbs
6 club or hero rolls
3 tablespoons butter or margarine, melted

1 Drain oysters; dry on paper toweling.
2 Beat egg with salt and pepper in a pie plate; sprinkle cracker crumbs in second pie plate. Dip oysters, one at a time, into egg mixture, then into crumbs; repeat with egg and crumbs to coat well.
3 Fry oysters, a few at a time, in about a 1-inch depth of fat heated to 380° in large frying pan, turning once, about 2 minutes, or until golden-brown. Drain on paper toweling. Keep hot in moderate oven (350°) until all are cooked.
4 Cut a slice across top of each roll; scoop out middle to make a boat-shape shell. Brush inside and lid with butter or margarine; arrange in a shallow baking pan; toast in heated oven 10 minutes.
5 Fill shells with oysters; serve hot with lemon wedges and tartare sauce or chili sauce.

Scallops Florentine

Bake at 425° for 10 minutes. Makes 4 servings

1 pound frozen sea scallops, slightly thawed
¼ cup bottled Italian salad dressing
1 package (12 ounces) frozen mushrooms
4 tablespoons (½ stick) butter or margarine
¼ cup water
1 package (10 ounces) frozen chopped spinach
4 tablespoons all-purpose flour
2 eggs, separated
¼ cup light cream or table cream
Few drops liquid red pepper seasoning

1 Toss scallops with salad dressing in a medium-size bowl.
2 Sauté mushrooms in 2 tablespoons of the butter or margarine, following label directions, in a large frying pan; remove and set aside for Step 6. (Set remaining 2 tablespoons butter or margarine aside for Step 5.)
3 Place scallops with dressing and water in same pan; cover. Simmer 5 minutes, or just until tender. Remove scallops and return to bowl; strain liquid from pan into a 2-cup measure; add water, if needed, to make 1½ cups.
4 Cook spinach, following label directions; drain well.
5 Melt remaining 2 tablespoons butter or margarine in a medium-size saucepan; stir in flour. Cook, stirring constantly, just until bubbly. Stir in scallop liquid; continue cooking and stirring until sauce thickens and boils 1 minute; remove from heat.
6 Beat egg yolks slightly in a small bowl; stir in a generous ½ cup of the hot mixture, then stir back into remaining mixture in pan. Cook, stirring constantly, 1 minute. Measure out ½

Ribbon Oyster Scallop is another sleight-of-hand classic making the most of canned and frozen food.

cup, then blend cream and liquid red pepper seasoning into remaining sauce in pan; stir in scallops and mushrooms.

7 Beat egg whites until they stand in firm peaks in a medium-size bowl; fold in the ½ cup sauce mixture.

8 Spoon scallop mixture into 4 scallop shells or individual baking dishes; spoon cooked spinach around edges and egg-white mixture on top.

9 Bake in hot oven (425°) 10 minutes, or until topping is puffy-golden.

Stir-Fried Scallops
Makes 4 servings

1 cup diagonally sliced carrots (½ inch thick)
1 pound sea scallops
1 cup diagonally sliced celery (½ inch thick)
1 tablespoon cornstarch
¾ cup water
2 tablespoons vegetable oil
1 teaspoon salt
1 clove of garlic, peeled
1 large onion, chopped (1 cup)
1 can (5 ounces) sliced bamboo shoots, well drained
1 tablespoon dry sherry
1 tablespoon soy sauce
1 envelope instant chicken broth
    OR: 1 teaspoon granulated chicken bouillon
½ teaspoon sugar
1 package (10 ounces) spinach, washed and trimmed

1 Parboil carrots and celery in boiling water in a medium-size saucepan 5 minutes; drain and dry with paper toweling; reserve.
2 Slice scallops into very thin circles with a sharp thin-bladed knife; pat dry with paper toweling; reserve.
3 Combine cornstarch with 2 tablespoons of the water in a cup; blend until smooth; reserve.
4 Heat a large heavy skillet until it sizzles when sprinkled with few drops of water; add 1 tablespoon of the oil; heat; stir in salt. Spear garlic with a fork; brown on all sides in oil in skillet; remove and discard.
5 Add scallops to skillet; cook, stirring very rapidly, ½ minute; push to one side. Add remaining 1 tablespoon oil and heat. Add, in order, onions, carrots, celery and bamboo shoots, cooking and stirring very rapidly, 2 minutes after each addition, then pushing to one side of skillet with scallops.
6 Make well in center of skillet; to this well, add remaining water, soy sauce, sherry, instant chicken broth and sugar; stir to mix. Cover; lower heat; simmer 3 minutes.
7 Add spinach; cover; cook 3 minutes longer, or until spinach wilts. Stir in cornstarch mixture; cook until mixture thickens, clears and boils 1 minute. Serve immediately over hot rice, if you wish.

●

Easy Coquilles St. Jacques
An easy gourmet dish—and it's pretty enough for a spring luncheon party.
Bake at 350° about 15 minutes. Makes 4 servings

5 tablespoons butter or margarine
½ cup soft bread crumbs (about 2 slices)

2 tablespoons Parmesan cheese
3 tablespoons chopped parsley
2 tablespoons chopped chives
3 tablespoons lemon juice
1 teaspoon Worcestershire sauce
1 pound (about 40) sea scallops
    OR: 2 packages (7 ounces each) frozen sea scallops
1 can (10½ ounces) condensed cream of celery soup

1 Melt butter or margarine in medium-size frying pan; toss 1 tablespoonful with bread crumbs and Parmesan cheese and save for Step 2; stir parsley, chives, lemon juice and Worcestershire sauce into remaining butter in pan; add fresh or frozen scallops; cover; simmer 8 to 10 minutes.
2 Divide cooked scallops among 4 buttered scallop shells or individual casseroles; stir soup into juices in frying pan; heat to boiling; pour sauce over scallops; top with Parmesan bread crumbs.
3 Bake in moderate oven (350°) 15 minutes, or just until crumbs are golden and sauce is bubbly-hot.

●

Cape Cod Scallop Salad
Another favorite from the sea goes high style with crisp vegetables in a creamy dressing.
Makes 4 servings

1 pound fresh or frozen sea scallops
2 tablespoons butter or margarine, melted
2 tablespoons bottled Italian salad dressing
1 tablespoon chopped parsley
½ teaspoon grated lemon peel
1 cup chopped celery
½ cup sliced radishes
¼ cup thinly sliced cucumber
¼ cup mayonnaise or salad dressing
1 head of lettuce

1 Wash fresh scallops under running cold water, or partly thaw frozen ones. Cut each in thin slices.
2 Coat slices well with melted butter or margarine in a large frying pan; cover; cook slowly 5 minutes.
3 Lift out with slotted spoon and place in a medium-size bowl; toss with Italian dressing, parsley and lemon rind; cover. Chill several hours to season and blend flavors.
4 Stir in celery, radishes, cucumber and mayonnaise or salad dressing.
5 Make nests of lettuce in 4 individual salad bowls or seashells. Spoon scallop salad into centers; garnish each with a "flower" of sliced cucumber, radish and ripe olive, if you wish.

INDEX TO RECIPES IN THIS VOLUME

1791

Ham Pinwheels 1703
Ham-Salad Triangles 1674
Hawaiian Bologna Buns 1694
Heidelbergs 1686
Hot Crab Salad Boats 1701
Hot Steak Bunwiches 1678
Italian-Sausage Heroes 1696
Jelly Roll-Ups 1710
Juarez Turkey Buns 1676
Liver-and-Bacon Boats 1698
Liver-and-Egg Boats 1698
Lobster Top Hats 1706
Meat Loaf Lineup 1676
Mediterranean Medley 1688
Melty Mix-Ups 1673
Milwaukee Jumbos 1677
Milwaukee Stack-Ups 1681
Miniature Salmon Eclairs 1706
Mint Jewels 1710
Mock Pizza Loaf 1686
Mushroom-Butter Rounds 1702
Orange Cream Crescents 1710
Oven Tuna Buns 1699
Oyster Pacesetters 1699
Pagoda Ham Cups 1703
Parsley-Cheese Filling 1708
Party Chicken Salad 1706
Pâté Supper Sandwiches 1674
Peanut-Butter Towers 1672
Pimiento-Cress Whirligigs 1708
Pocketbook Hotdogs 1677
Ribbon Rosies 1708
Ribbon Sandwich Cake 1702
Rivieras 1676
Salmon Salad 1707
Ship-a-Heroes 1696
Simple Salmon Jumbos 1679
Smorgasbord Sandwiches 1684
Souffléed Ham Whoppers 1689
Steak Medallions 1686
Steak Rolls 1679
Strawberry Cornucopias 1710
Stroganoff Subs 1693
Stuffed Ham Slices 1693
Stuffed Salad Rolls 1693
Sun-Glow Salad 1687
Super Burgers 1676
Super Subs 1695
Supper Sandwich 1696
Surprise Sandwiches 1690
Tijuana Toasties 1689
Triangle Crisps 1673
Twin Dagwoods on a Skewer 1681
Vienna Heroes 1694
Watercress Whirls 1709
Western Tuna Buns 1699
Whopper Heroes 1697
Zigzag Sandwich Loaf 1683

Garnishes:
Carrot Curls 1764
Dilled Cucumber Crisps 1687

1792

Sauces and Gravies:
Almond Butter 1715
Anchovy Sauce 1714
Barbecue Sauce 1723
Basic Gravy 1713
Basic Medium White Sauce 1714
Basic Thick White Sauce 1714
Basic Thin White Sauce 1714
Béarnaise Sauce 1717
Blue-Cheese Sauce 1716
Bright Seafood Dip 1743
Brown Butter (Beurre Noir) 1715
Brown Butter Amandine 1715
Brown Butter Piquant 1715
Brown Butter Sauce 1715
Brown Butter Sesame 1716
Caesar Sauce 1716
Caper Sauce 1721
Caraway-Cheese Sauce 1728
Caraway Cream 1716
Caribbean Sauce 1726
Cheese Sauce 1714
Chili Butter 1715
Chili-Cheese Sauce 1714
Chinese Sweet-Sour Sauce 1727
Chive-Cheese Sauce 1728
Chive-Sour Cream Sauce 1716
Chrysanthemum Soy Sauce 1768
Crab and Shrimp Sauce 1762
Creamy Caper Sauce 1716
Creamy Curry Sauce 1724
Creamy Egg Sauce 1735
Cucumber Cream 1716
Cucumber Dip 1742
Cumberland Sauce 1720
Currant Jelly Glaze 1716
Curry Butter 1715
Curry Cream 1716
Curry à la Crème 1726
Curry Dip 1779
Curry Sauce 1721
Dark Cherry Sauce 1723
Deviled Egg Sauce 1716
Dill Butter 1724
Dill Cream 1726
Easy Dill Sauce 1747
Egg-Caper Sauce 1744
Exotic Herb Sauce 1714
Figaro Sauce 1725
Fluffy Hollandaise Sauce 1724
Fresh Tartare Sauce 1743
Garlic Butter 1715
Ginger-Marmalade Glaze 1717
Goldenrod Sauce 1726
Gourmet White Sauce 1726
Guacamole Sauce 1726
Herb Butter 1715
Herbed Egg Sauce 1727
Hollandaise Sauce 1736
Horseradish-Almond Sauce 1718
Horseradish Cream 1716
Hot Dip 1780

Hot-Hot Mustard 1766
Italian Tomato Sauce 1720
Javanese Peanut Sauce 1720
Leek Sauce 1786
Mandarin Meat Sauce 1718
Mandarin-Raisin Sauce 1718
Mayonnaise Sauce 1716
Mock Béarnaise Sauce 1717
Mock Hollandaise 1725
Mornay Sauce 1714
Mousseline Sauce 1724
Mushroom-Diable Sauce 1718
Mustard Butter 1715
Mustard Sauce 1720
New Delhi Cream 1714
Newburg Sauce 1723
Old-Fashioned Cheese Sauce 1714
Old-Time Brown Sugar Glaze
    1716
Olive-Chive Cream 1728
Olive Sauce 1748
Olive Sauce-Gravy 1720
Onion Cream 1726
Orange-Honey Glaze 1716
Orange-Mint Sauce 1721
Paprika Butter 1715
Parmesan Butter 1715
Parmesan Sauce 1715
Pecan Butter 1715
Peppy Guacamole Sauce 1765
Pimiento Cheese Sauce 1728
Pineapple-Curry Glaze 1716
Pink Sauce 1714
Pink Zip 1727
Plum Sauce 1723
Polonaise Sauce 1727
Puffed Derby Sauce 1716
Quick Bordelaise Sauce 1718
Radish Cream 1729
Relish Cream 1726
Savory Butter Sauce 1715
Savory Egg Sauce 1756
Savory Mustard 1726
Shallot Butter 1715
Shrimp Newburg Sauce 1770
Sour Cream Sauce 1716
Spicy Plum Sauce 1766
Spring Egg Sauce 1714
Springtime Sauce 1725
Stroganoff Sauce 1721
Supreme Sauce 1722
Swiss-Cheese Sauce 1784
Swiss Tartare Sauce 1724
Tart Tartare Sauce 1735
Tartare Sauce 1724
Tomato-Cheese Sauce 1714
Watercress Cream 1727
Worcestershire Butter 1715
Zippy Hot Mustard Cream 1716

Pies and Pastries:
Pastry Shell 1748